CHOSEN
FAMILIES

Chosen Families

With Read-Aloud Section for Children,
Who Am I? Who Are My Parents?

KAY MARSHALL STROM

PYRANEE
BOOKS

Zondervan Publishing House
Grand Rapids, Michigan

CHOSEN FAMILIES

This is a Pyranee Book
Published by the Zondervan Publishing House
1415 Lake Drive S.E., Grand Rapids, Michigan 49506

Copyright © 1985 by The Zondervan Corporation

Library of Congress Cataloging in Publication Data

Strom, Kay Marshall, 1943–
    Chosen families.
    "With read-aloud section for children: Who am I? Who are my parents?"
    Pyranee books.
    Bibliography: p.
    1. Adoption—United States—Case studies. I. Title.
HV875.55.S76   1985   362.7'34   85-3256
ISBN 0-310-33591-4

Unless otherwise indicated, the Scripture text used is *The Living Bible*, copyright © 1971 by Tyndale House Publishers, Wheaton, Illinois.

The pronouns *he* and *she* are sometimes used generically and interchangeably where the gender is insignificant.

Edited by Lisa Garvelink
Designed by Ann Cherryman

Printed in the United States of America

87 88 89 90 / 10 9 8 7

CONTENTS

WHO AM I?
WHO ARE MY PARENTS?

PREFACE

Homeless children. Caring adults. Drawn together by love and united by adoption, they can become families—real families in which each member is accepted and respected for who he is.

Some of you have already expanded your families with one or more adopted children. Congratulations! You have chosen to increase your family in the same way that God increases His. Others of you are just beginning to explore this possibility. It will be exciting to see what God has in store for you.

Before you read further in this book, I want to tell you something about my own family. My husband Larry and I are the parents of two children. Fifteen-year-old Lisa is petite, brown-eyed, and interested in anything musical. Eric, who is twelve, is a tall, slender blond, always on the go. They are nothing alike in appearance or personality, nor do they share the same interests or abilities. They are not much like their parents, either. But Lisa and Eric are not adopted. Both were born to Larry and me.

Not only am I not an adoptive parent, but I wasn't even an adopted child myself. So why am I writing this book? What right have I to speak on the subject? Actually, I'm speaking on the very best of authority—the experiences of almost fifty adoptive families.

In the chapters that follow you will be sharing in the lives and deeply emotional experiences of these adoptive families, so it is good for you to know something about them. They run the gamut from a retired couple in their late sixties to a couple in their early thirties who, after years of waiting, have just recently welcomed a two-month-old baby into their home. Included among the families are many national backgrounds and diverse lifestyles: doctors and lawyers; secretaries and a librarian; construction workers, an artist, and a musician; teachers, homemakers, engineers; business men and women, a pilot, and a farmer. Some families are well-to-do while others are struggling to make ends meet.

These families represent many different adoptive situations.

Some adopted through adoption agencies while others chose independent adoptions. Some adopted children from overseas. A few have chosen to accept hard-to-place children—those who are older or who have a physical, mental, or emotional handicap. Some, because of death or divorce, are adoptive stepparents. Two are single parents. Many have very happy or deeply moving experiences to relate, but there are a few who, through tears, share in this book the bitterness and pain that the adoption has brought.

Despite their differences, the people I interviewed all have two things in common: each is a Christian adoptive parent, and each has an important story to tell. Although their stories are unique, it is interesting to note the threads of similarity that run through them all.

As I interviewed these families and listened as they related their adoptive experiences, I was struck by the sharply differing points of reference. "Adoption is the only way to go!" announced one obviously satisfied father. "I don't think that any family is really complete without an adopted child!" But another stated, "If we had it to do again, my wife and I would remain childless." One parent shook her head and sighed, "There are so many problems with an adopted child," while another happily claimed, "Problems? We haven't had any. If you want my opinion, people make their own problems."

Had any of these families chosen to write a book on adoption, it would almost certainly have been based on their own experiences and therefore would have reflected their own situation—perhaps overly negative, perhaps overly positive, perhaps just narrow in scope. It is only by basing a book on the combined experiences of many families that we can hope to achieve a relatively objective, overall picture of the adoptive experience. My hope and prayer is that this has been achieved in this book and that in the following pages many of you will find a source of help and encouragement. Perhaps you will even discover that special place in the adoptive circle into which you can fit.

I am gratefully indebted to each of the adoptive mothers and fathers who shared their experiences with me. Without them there would be no book. To each of them I say, "Thank you." I was fortunate as well to have had the help, advice, suggestions, and criticism of many professionals who are intimately acquainted with the tough realities of adoption today. Two who were especially helpful were Douglas Donnelly, attorney at law, and Dr. Samuel McDill, licensed family counselor. Their time, interest, and expertise were invaluable in the completion of this book.

As you read this book, I ask that you do so prayerfully. Answer the questions at the end of each chapter thoughtfully. It is my earnest desire and prayer that you discover your own personal answer to the question, "Is there, somewhere, a child for me?"

CHOSEN
FAMILIES

1. *Is There a Child for You?*

"Shortly after our marriage Patrick and I saw a television documentary on the plight of homeless children," said Laura Reid. "That started us thinking. We could either build our own family by bringing children into the world as our parents did, or we could choose to provide a loving Christian home for children who are already living. We decided on the latter. All of our children were to be adopted."

"After Ginger endured three miscarriages and an endless string of tests, the doctor broke the news to us that she would never be able to bear a child," said Bert Delgado. "We had already discussed the possibility of adoption, but now it's time for us to check into it seriously. We need to see exactly what our options are."

"My husband and I have three natural children," said Corrine Borowitz, "but we want more. Both Stephen and I have always wanted lots of kids—at least five or six. Adoption seems the perfect way for us to complete our family."

Life is made up of a progression of decisions. We all have to make them. Like the Reids, the Delgados, and the Borowitzes, many of you have made or will be making a decision about the adoption of a child. You are not alone. There are approximately two-and-a-half million adoptees in the United States, and every one of them represents a similar decision made by their adoptive parents.

Unless you are just beginning to consider adoption, you have probably heard and read conflicting and discouraging reports about what can be expected. You may be feeling frustrated, confused, or simply uninformed. Perhaps you have already adopted, but now you are faced with hard problems and difficult questions for which you feel unprepared. If you fit into either of these categories, this book will help you.

What is adoption? Very simply, it means taking a child

who was not born to you and making him your own. It is a legal process governed by the particular laws of your specific state (see appendix 1). But there is more. Adoption is also an emotional process governed by your heart. This is how it is expressed in the Talmud:

> A mother is likened to a mountain spring that nourishes the tree at the root. But one who mothers another's child is likened unto a water that rises into a cloud and goes a long distance to nourish a lone tree in the desert.

It used to be that the emphasis in adoption was put on finding children for childless couples—almost always upper-middle income, well-educated, Anglo-Saxon families. Fortunately that has changed. Today the emphasis is on the child and what is best for him. Every child has a right to loving parents, to the security of belonging, and to a permanent place in a family of his own.

WHAT DO I HAVE TO OFFER?

So the place to start your consideration of adoption is with yourself. What do you have to offer a child? I don't mean material things: money and clothes and toys and private schools. I mean the basic necessities like love, understanding, guidance, acceptance, security, and the firm foundation that only comes from a well-grounded faith in God. It takes a strong, mature, secure person to be a good parent. Do you qualify? These questions might help you decide:

- Do my family and I want to make a lifelong commitment to a child?
- Does my spouse want a child as much as I do?
- Do I have a happy, stable marriage flexible enough to include a child?
- Can I truly love and accept a child who was not born to me? Can I allow him to be himself, whatever that might be?
- Can I love this child through the bad times as well as the good times?
- Can I be reasonable in my expectations for my child?

Can I accept his failures no matter how big and praise his successes no matter how small?

- If I decide to accept an older child can I wait patiently for him to love and accept me? Do I understand that this may take quite a while?
- Can I talk honestly with my child about his adoption?
- Will I be able to accept and honestly answer his questions about his biological parents without feeling threatened or defensive?

Now let us consider another list. These are some excellent reasons *not* to adopt a child:

- Do I feel that an adopted child would be second best, not really like my own?
- Would I always be embarrassed about the fact that my child was adopted?
- Do I fear that my adopted child would repeat the mistakes and carry on the problems of his biological parents?
- Do I feel that adopting a needy, homeless child is my moral duty? Do I see myself as a rescuer?
- Have I already decided who and what I want my child to be? Would I have trouble accepting a child whose abilities and interests were different from my expectations?

We must understand and accept the fact that no child ever comes with a guarantee. Our precious baby may grow up to be lazy, stubborn, dull, rebellious, or ugly. This is true of biological children no less than adopted children. Somehow, natural parents seem to have less trouble adjusting to such unexpected traits than adoptive parents do. But the fact is, adoptive parenthood brings with it the very same ups and downs, joys and disappointments as biological parenthood. And there are extra challenges as well.

No one expects us to be perfect parents. There is no such thing. Like children, parents are individuals. Every one of them has problems and personality flaws. The most important consideration is that the adoptive parents be able to meet the physical and emotional needs of their child.

Just what are the needs of a child? Unfortunately there is no single right answer to the question, because needs vary from child to child. There are, however, some universals.

- All infants' physical needs must be met. Infants are totally dependent on others for their survival and well-being.
- From infancy onward, children need good examples on which to base their own actions. They are learning constantly, and what they learn depends on what they see.
- Children need the love and care of an adult whom they can trust and who will give them security. Without this they will grow up severely handicapped when it comes time to form other relationships in life.
- To develop to their full potential, children need to be raised in an atmosphere of acceptance. They need to be appreciated for who and what they are.

These needs are the same for all children, adopted or not. In fact, there are not nearly so many differences between the two groups as we might imagine. Birth families and adoptive families alike must endure the trials and tribulations of everyday life. Broken bones, temper tantrums, diaper rashes, spilled milk, crying and pouting, sibling rivalry, wet beds, bouts with the flu, disappointing report cards, piano lessons, joys, love, hate, hurts, laughter—they happen to all of us. They are a part of life. Every family has crises and problems, strengths and weaknesses, good times and bad.

Yet adoptive families do face pressures and problems and questions that other families know nothing about. Even when adopted children grow up in a secure, loving family, they still need to gain some understanding of why they were given up for adoption in the first place. They, and their adoptive parents as well, need to recognize and accept both their birth backgrounds and their adoption as part of their identity.

Adopted children are certain to have questions about their birth parents (see chapter 11). At times they will feel different and wonder if they belong at all. This may cause you to think that you were a failure as a parent and that your child doesn't love you. That is not true. His questions and anxieties are simply a part of growing up. Over the years your child has learned to trust you, and when he is in need of help and support it is to you that he will turn. After all, you are his parent.

When we think of adoption, we tend to think of childless couples who choose babies very similar in appearance to what their own biological children might be. If this is the only adoptive situation you will accept, you can expect to wait a very long time. Today there are few healthy infants available for adoption. But that is not to say that there is a shortage of adoptive children. There isn't. Minority and mixed-race children are available (chapter 5). So are children with physical, mental, or emotional handicaps (chapter 6). There are older children, and there are siblings who must be placed together (chapter 7). So even if a newborn baby is not available to you, or if you are not interested in one, there may still be a child for you.

In the past it was next to impossible for an unmarried person to adopt a child. Today more and more children are being placed with single parents (chapter 10). Also, as divorce and remarriage continue to increase, so do the number of adoptions by stepparents (chapter 10).

If, after considering all the alternatives, you decide that you really are not interested in adopting any child other than a healthy newborn, don't let anyone influence you differently. It is far better to resign yourself to a long wait, or even to never getting a baby at all, than to adopt a child out of desperation. If you do that, you may never be able to really love and accept that child. So listen to yourself. You must do what is right for you.

"HOW CAN WE PREPARE?"

"We think we want to adopt," said a thirty-one-year-old wife of ten years, "but neither my husband nor I have had any experience with children. How can we best prepare ourselves to make a wise decision?"

This is a good question that many thoughtful couples ask. There are many child-oriented activities in which you can become involved—scouts, athletic coaching, Sunday school teaching, or church nursery volunteering—but these all offer very limited exposure. An ideal approach is to become a foster parent for a child who needs temporary care (chapter 8). In most areas of the country there is a continuing need for such homes.

Adoption can be a rewarding and challenging experience. What an opportunity to help a child move toward the development of his particular abilities and his unique personality!

But parenting is never an easy job. Along with the wonderfully rewarding times come the times of questions and nagging doubts. Worst of all are the times when our only feeling is one of failure. Perhaps because they have gone through so much to become parents in the first place, adoptive parents seem to be especially vulnerable to the concerns and questions of parenting.

To provide some concrete help, advice, and comfort to Christian adoptive parents, I called together representatives from the two groups of people who have the most to offer them: trained professionals and parents who have been there. Ten couples met together with a Christian family counselor and a Christian attorney to discuss some of the most common problems and concerns of adoptive parenthood. Portions of this open forum, presented in dialogue form, are included in many of the following chapters.

The professionals who participated in this discussion were Dr. Samuel R. McDill, a family counselor in private practice in Santa Barbara, California, and Douglas R. Donnelly, a lawyer practicing in the same city who is also the father of two adopted daughters. Except for these two men, all the names used in the book are fictitious.

To further protect the privacy of the families who graciously shared their experiences with me, all the accounts presented here are composites. All the situations are true experiences of the adoptive families, but none will be able to point to a specific family in the book and say, "That's us." Parts of a situation are drawn from one family, other parts from someone else.

This book will show that there are a number of adoptive options open to you. Read about the needs and the rewards each option presents, but also consider the difficulties. If you decide to adopt, you must go into the relationship with your eyes open. Be prepared for love, fulfillment, and a great blessing. They will come. But also be prepared for problems and for disappointments. They will also come.

As you can see, an adopted family is, in every sense of the term, a *real* family.

QUESTIONS FOR DISCUSSION

1. In your opinion is the shift in the emphasis of adoption from the needs of childless couples to the needs of the children good or bad? Why?
2. In making the decision whether or not to adopt a child, what should be the most important considerations?
3. In what ways are birth families and adoptive families alike? In what ways are they different?

2. Adoption: Whose Choice?

It was the first day of school, and Mrs. Martin, the sixth-grade teacher, was getting acquainted with the students in her class. When Tom and Stephen Jamison introduced themselves as brothers, Mrs. Martin could scarcely hide her amazement. Stephen, tall and thin, had sandy-blond hair and a freckle-covered face; Tom was short and husky with a headful of unruly black curls.

"Surely you boys aren't twins!" Mrs. Martin exclaimed.

"Oh, no," Stephen replied. "I'm five months older than Tom."

"Yeah," Tom agreed. Then he added, "One of us is adopted, but I forget which one."

The boys' casual attitude toward adoption made such an impression on their teacher that she decided to make it a point to meet their parents and see for herself what kind of a family could foster such open-minded acceptance in their children.

When Mrs. Jamison visited her sons' classroom later that week, Mrs. Martin greeted her warmly. "I can't tell you how impressed I am with your boys!" she exclaimed. "It's wonderful to see a family in which adoption makes no difference at all."

"I'm afraid that you don't understand," said Mrs. Jamison quickly. "Adoption makes a great deal of difference in our family. In fact, it has been a regular part of our conversation since our sons were toddlers. You see, we are all adopted—my husband and me, Tom and Stephen—all of us." Noticing the teacher's puzzled look, Mrs. Jamison explained, "We are Christians. Each of us has been adopted by God into His family so that now we're all His children. It's God Himself who is the model for our attitude toward adoption."

What understanding the Jamison family had! Not only was adoption an important fact of life for them, but it was a vital part of their religious faith as well. As His adopted sons and daughters, all Christians are truly the children of God. What a complete and perfect family relationship!

In his letter to the Galatians, the apostle Paul says,

> But when the right time came, the time God decided on, He sent His Son, born of a woman, born as a Jew, to buy freedom for us who were slaves to the law so that He could adopt us as His very own sons. And because we are His sons, God has sent the Spirit of His Son into our hearts, so now we can rightly speak of God as our dear Father (Galatians 4:4–6).

Can there be a more perfect example for adoptive parents?

In God's eyes, every Christian is so completely a part of His family that each one shares equally in all its rights, privileges, and responsibilities. Paul adds, "Now we are no longer slaves, but God's own sons. And since we are His sons, everything He has belongs to us, for that is the way God planned it" (Galatians 4:7). We share a wonderful legacy.

Can you imagine such a thing as a second-class member of God's family? Of course not! Every one of His children is equal in His sight. The same equality should be present in every Christian family, adoptive or not. It is inevitable that children will be influenced by the attitudes and prejudices of their parents. If adoptive parents feel that they have somehow failed by not being able to bring children into the world, why should they be surprised when their adopted children consider themselves second-best? It is hard to feel like a first-class person when your parents consider you a consolation prize.

Even when parents accept the idea of adoption from God's perspective, there are sure to be friends and relatives who do not understand. But with prayer, careful teaching, and a consistent example, these children will be able to withstand the thoughtlessness of others.

"Once when our boys were little," said Mrs. Jamison, "Stephen got a birthday present from my sister. On the card she had written, 'Happy birthday from your adopted Aunt Margaret.' After Stephen read it he said, 'I never knew that Aunt Margaret was adopted.'" Stephen was secure in his position as a worthy member of the family. He belonged and he knew it.

Is it realistic to expect to be able to love an adopted child in

23

the same way that we love a natural child? Consider how Mrs. Jamison expressed her relationship to her two sons:

> Tom was born to us, so he's our son. Stephen was born to another woman but we adopted him, so he's our son. The two boys entered our family in different ways, one physically and the other legally. Only a mother who has borne a child can fully understand the wonder of birth, and only one who has adopted can fully understand the miracle that makes an adopted child her own. How fortunate I am to have experienced both miracles and to know that they are really not so very different after all! The different ways in which our boys came into our family make no difference at all. They were both given to us by God and we love them both the same.

Every child in the world is a separate little person—an individual with her own potential, her own problems, her own unique characteristics, her own personality. We are told in the Holy Scriptures that God has a perfect plan for each of His children and a reason for everything that happens in their lives. The psalmist said, "You saw me before I was born and scheduled each day of my life before I began to breathe. Every day was recorded in your book!" (Psalm 139:16). And in Romans 8:28 we read, "And we know that all that happens to us is working for our good if we love God and are fitting into His plans."

How wonderful it is to know that God has personally chosen one very special child and has placed her in a very special home for a very special reason. There is no luck involved—no fate, no chance. The arrangements are all in the hands of God.

Although a child is born with certain abilities, talents, and potential, there is no question but that she is greatly influenced by the way she is raised. What she learns at home goes a long way toward helping to determine who and what she will become. Potential—no matter how great—means nothing without the daily example of dedicated parents.

This is a great challenge to us as parents. We must help our children to realize and develop their own potential; we must help to direct them in such a way that when God needs them, they will be ready and willing to do His bidding. God alone knows what is possible with the perfect combination of your home and that specific life He has entrusted to your care.

Do you feel inadequate for this task? Don't! God also sets us an example as the Ideal Parent. He is loving and kind, patient and just. When we do wrong, He chastises us in love. But He is also merciful and always willing to forgive. God promised that when He calls us to meet the needs of our children, His grace will be sufficient for us (2 Corinthians 12:9). He will enable us to do what He has called us to do.

TRIUMPHANT EXAMPLES IN THE BIBLE

Have you ever noticed how many stories there are in the Bible about children who were removed from the homes of their birth and raised by others? It is noteworthy that in most cases the story begins as a tragedy, but in the end stands as a triumphant example of God's sovereignty over all things. Let's look at a few of these displaced children and see how God in His great wisdom changed each tragedy into a life of victory.

Joseph was seventeen when he was sold by his jealous brothers and taken as a slave to the faraway country of Egypt. Surely this was the most bitter tragedy that could befall Joseph and his father Jacob. Yet years later, Joseph, looking back on his long, often difficult life, said to his brothers, "As far as I am concerned, God turned into good what you meant for evil, for He brought me to this high position I have today so that I could save the lives of many people" (Genesis 50:20). And it was the descendants of Jacob, brought to Egypt by Joseph and so saved from sure starvation, who grew into the great nation of Israel. Had Joseph remained at home with his father, there would never have been an Israel through which Jesus, the Savior of the world, would come.

As the years passed, pharaohs who had never known Joseph ascended the throne of Egypt. Conditions grew worse and worse for God's people. Finally they were forced into cruel slavery, where they led a wretched and miserable existence. But there were so many Israelites that the Egyptians began to fear lest they should revolt and take over the land. So the pharaoh issued a decree that every male born to an Israelite woman was to be thrown into the Nile River to drown. It was at this time of crisis that Moses was born. As far as we know, only this baby—floating down the Nile in a little reed boat made by his mother—managed to survive the deadly decree. By the intervention of the all-powerful hand of God, Moses lived to become the greatest leader Israel ever knew—the person God chose to lead the exodus of His people from Egyptian captivity.

Esther was a beautiful Jewish girl who lived with her cousin Mordecai. They were captives in the heathen land of Persia: Imagine her feelings when she was ordered to become one of the wives of the vain, powerful, and sometimes brutal Persian king! In time, a terrible death plot was laid for the Jewish population of Persia. Queen Esther alone was in a position to intervene with the king on behalf of the Jews, knowing if she were to do so, it would mean placing her own life in danger. As she struggled with this momentous decision, Mordecai came to her and said, "Who can say but that God has brought you into the palace for just such a time as this?" (Esther 4:14). Esther had her answer. "I will go in to see the king; and if I perish, I perish." You remember what happened. Esther was graciously received by the king, and because of her brave action the Jews in Persia were saved from genocide.

Perhaps you are saying, "But my adopted child will never be a Joseph or a Moses or an Esther." You are probably right. God chooses few people for such history-changing assignments as He gave them. Yet you can be certain that God has chosen your child for unique service to Him. Your child is being prepared in your home to meet God's challenge for her life. In God's perfect opinion, no one can raise that child as well as you, the parents He has selected for the task. Remember, parenting does not just mean conceiving a child, but also raising one. It is a singular privilege. It is a singular responsibility.

EXAMINE YOUR MOTIVES

A word of warning is necessary. If you are a Christian who is considering adoption you must prayerfully, in complete honesty, examine your reasons for wanting to take a child into your home and heart. This is a crucial decision for you and the child, and you dare not enter into it lightly.

"I want a baby of my own more than I've ever wanted anything in my life," said the thirty-year-old wife of a successful banker. "Yet after ten years of marriage there still is no baby. My husband and I have been to specialist after specialist, but they haven't been able to help us. One doctor did tell me that when a couple adopts a baby it often happens that they soon have one of their own. I can't understand how this would work, but after ten years of waiting, I'm willing to try anything."

A twenty-six-year-old secretary, married for five years, nervously told me, "I hate to admit it, but my marriage is on pretty shaky ground. Lately I've been thinking about adopting a baby because I'm sure that a baby would draw my husband and me back together. It would give us a common interest. With a new baby, maybe we would have a chance to be a real family after all."

"Whenever I read a story about a family who adopts little children no one else wants, I get a warm feeling inside," said a twenty-two-year-old wife of three years. "I think it would be fun to adopt. What I have in mind is two little girls, one blond with blue eyes and the other a brunette with big brown eyes. I can almost see them now—all dressed up in pretty ruffled dresses, their long curls tied up in ribbons. My husband laughs at me, but I know he will agree. He's always saying that I need something to keep me busy."

Do these reasons for wanting to adopt sound incredible? Unfortunately, they aren't uncommon. It is surprising how many people seem to forget that a baby is not a doll, but a real live human being who gets dirty and cries and grows into a stubborn child who stomps her foot and yells, "I hate you!" Any couple who decides to take a child in order to satisfy a romantic idea of having a real live doll to cuddle and dress up and show off is being terribly unfair to all concerned. Inevitably those who adopt in the hopes of increasing their chances of having "their own" baby or of saving a troubled marriage will soon find that parenthood is not the magic solution they had thought it would be.

Take the time to consider carefully. Discuss your motives openly with your spouse. Pray together. Do you automatically assume that children are a necessity for a married couple? Do you want a son to carry on your family name? Do you have to talk a reluctant spouse into agreeing to the adoption? Do you want a child to take the place of one who died? None of these is an adequate reason for adopting. Only when a couple has a true, God-given desire to take a child into their home and to make him their very own—to provide that child with a warm, secure, understanding, loving, and nurturing family—can an adoption be successful. The adopted child, like any other child, must be loved and wanted and appreciated for himself, not for what he can do for his parents.

"My husband and I love each other very much," said an energetic mother of two adopted daughters. "In a way the two of us were already a complete family, but we so wanted children with whom we could share our love. Together we prayed that God would either give us the baby we wanted so badly, or else take away our great desire to be parents. But instead of fading, our deep longing for a child continued to grow, so we were convinced that this desire was truly from the Lord." Then, her eyes sparkling, she gazed out the window into the backyard where her two preschoolers were playing in the sandbox. "Do you want proof of God's faithfulness?" she asked. "Just look at the two wonderful, healthy, bright little girls He gave us!"

THE UNIQUENESS OF CHRISTIAN ADOPTION

A Christian view of adoption, then, is unique in several ways. It is a concept authored by God and demonstrated by Him in its most perfect and complete sense by His adoption of all Christian believers into His own family. It is the providential choosing of a very special child selected above all other children to be placed in a very special family for a very special purpose. It is a calling—a divine appointment—from the Lord God Himself.

"I have a poem by Fleur Conkling Heylinger that I claim as my own," said Mrs. Jamison, the mother of Tom and Stephen. "It's special to me because it expresses so well what I have always felt in my heart. It could have been written by me. Will you please share it with other adoptive parents?"

Here is the poem:

> To an Adopted Child
>
> Not flesh of my flesh,
> Nor bone of my bone,
> But still miraculously my own.
> Never forget for a single minute,
> You didn't grow under my heart,
> You grew in it!
>
> Fleur Conkling Heylinger

QUESTIONS FOR DISCUSSION

1. The analogy drawn between God's adoption of His children and the Christian's adoption of earthly children is sound. However, there are differences (because all analogies break down if carried far enough). In what ways is human adoption different from divine adoption?
2. To what extent do you feel that you can and should expect God to choose a specific child for your family?

3. *The Classic Story*

"All along, Dan and I had planned for the day when we would have a family," said Ellen O'Brien. A slender, soft-spoken woman of thirty-three, Ellen paused for a moment, silently remembering. "We were young and idealistic then. We had our whole lives planned out. I was going to teach for two years while Dan finished graduate school. By then I would be pregnant, and—according to our plan—by the time the baby was born Dan would be set up in his own accounting office and I would have retired from teaching. Two years later there would be a second baby and two years after that we would complete our family with a third. It all seemed so perfect.

"But God had plans of His own. After five years I still had not conceived. Together we went to see a doctor who specialized in fertility problems. After endless tests and weeks of waiting, he broke the news to us. I would never be able to have a baby. What a terrible shock! All our plans and dreams and hopes— gone in a minute! I cried all the way home.

"Dan was terribly shaken too. In fact, he refused to believe it. 'Our God is a God of miracles,' he said. 'We will take this matter up with Him.' So we prayed and prayed and prayed. We carefully pointed out to God our excellent qualifications for parenthood. We promised to dedicate the baby to Him. Again and again we reminded God of His promise to give us the desires of our heart. Sometimes I felt certain that God was going to answer us and give us a baby. At other times I wondered in despair if He even heard us. Those were horribly frustrating days for both of us.

"After two long years of tearful praying and pleading with God, Dan and I began to think about the possibility of adopting. The more we discussed it, the more certain we became that this was the way God would answer our prayers. He was going to give us our baby, all right, but it was to be according to His plan, not ours.

"Together Dan and I filled out an application at our local adoption agency and, with great excitement and anticipation, we turned it in. Although we were certain of our guidance from God, the agency apparently was not. We received a long, official letter from them. What it really said was: 'Don't call us, we'll call you—in about two years!' "

Dan and Ellen O'Brien had gone to the agency knowing exactly what they wanted: a healthy, white infant. They were not interested in any child who did not fit this description. Most couples have the same expectations as the O'Briens, so the demand for these babies is much greater than the supply.

"Just nine months after we talked to the lady at the adoption agency, we got a call," Ellen continued. "They already had a baby for us! I was so excited that I spent the next two days on the phone making our happy announcement to relatives and friends. We chose names—Jessica Hope for a girl, Jeremy Sean for a boy. That weekend we papered and painted the nursery, and I ordered furniture for it. Then I went shopping and bought piles of baby clothes and a fuzzy bear that played Brahms' Lullaby when it was wound up. There would be no hand-me-downs for our little Jessica or Jeremy. We were going first-class all the way.

"Then came the shattering blow. The baby was born right on time, a perfect little boy. But when we arrived at the hospital to get him, he was gone. His natural grandmother had suddenly appeared out of nowhere and claimed him as her own. There was nothing we could do about it. We had no rights; she was a blood relative. It was as if our baby, born strong and healthy, had suddenly died. My heart was broken.

"For the first time, Dan and I realized that if there were ever going to be an O'Brien baby, it would have to be because God had given it to us. This was a hard thing for us to admit. We had always believed that the two of us together could solve any problems that might come into our lives. We prided ourselves on our own sufficiency. Everything that was important to us—education, a new home, a nice savings account—we had worked hard for and achieved. But now we were faced with a situation over which we had absolutely no control, a situation in

31

which we had to depend on God in a totally new way. He had put this desire in our hearts for a baby; we knew that He, in His own time and in His own way, would satisfy it.

"And do you know what? Just six months later we got Heather." Ellen's eyes sparkled with pride as she spoke of her little daughter. "What an answer God gave us! I surely am glad that He didn't listen to my advice."

Ellen and Dan's story could be echoed with only minor variations by the majority of adoptive parents across the United States. In general they are educated, financially secure people. Unable to have children, they decided to adopt. The child each couple wanted was a newborn baby who looked as much like them as possible. Since people who live closely together tend to pick up each other's habits and mannerisms, these parents and the children they adopted often have a remarkable family resemblance. They walk and talk alike, their expressions and gestures are alike, they even think and act alike. To all appearances, these families are no different from any other families.

Now, suppose a couple has thoughtfully and prayerfully made the decision to adopt. What is the next step? Dan and Ellen O'Brien made application through a state-licensed adoption agency, but in many states it is also possible to arrange an independent adoption (see appendix 1). Which option is better? There is no simple answer, because there are advantages and disadvantages to each approach.

AGENCY ADOPTIONS

In an agency adoption, the biological parents give up all rights to their child and trust the agency to find the best possible home for her. Because the baby is surrendered and the agency makes all the necessary arrangements, there is a likelihood that the identity of the biological parents will be kept confidential.

Couples or single people who have an application accepted at an adoption agency are assigned to a social worker who will serve them throughout the entire procedure. The social worker will counsel and help the prospective parents and will evaluate their readiness to adopt a child. Since social workers have had training in psychology, human development, and counseling, they can provide more than just information about the legal process of adoption. They are also able to offer support and guidance. If the social worker feels that the couple is not ready to adopt, or that they want to adopt for the wrong reasons, a child will not be placed in their home.

In their anxiety about the possibility of being turned down, many prospective parents make a big mistake. They try to guess what the social worker wants to hear and adjust their answers accordingly. It is absolutely essential that prospective parents be open and honest with their social worker. Remember, his only concern is the benefit of the child.

Nevertheless, much does depend on the social worker's impressions. How can prospective parents deal in the best way with this very important person? The following suggestions come from several social workers who have had a great deal of experience with adoptive parents.

- First of all, relax! Don't be afraid. The social worker is not trying to trap you.
- Always be honest. If you have strong feelings about something, state them.
- If you are confused, ask for clarification. If you have a question, ask it.
- Don't try to convince the social worker that you are a perfect person or that you would be a perfect parent. There is no such thing, and the social worker knows it.
- If you have doubts, don't hide them. Let the social worker help you work them out.
- Feel free to disagree with the social worker, but do so in a kind, pleasant way. Explain your point of view; it may be that you're right.
- Insist on being given all the information that is available concerning any child placed in your home. The time will come when you will be glad you have it.
- If your application is turned down, ask for an explanation. It may be that you really are not ready to take this step at this time.

To spare families the anguish that Dan and Ellen O'Brien suffered when their baby was claimed by his grandmother, an agency will usually place a newborn infant in a foster home until all questions regarding its legal relinquishment are cleared up. It may take several months to find the right home for the baby. Today many people object to a baby's spending these very important first weeks and months of life in a foster home.

In addition to these safeguards, most agencies are prepared and equipped to provide counseling and other specific assistance that is not generally available to parents who adopt privately.

There are many families who are not able to adopt through an agency because of the strict rules and regulations. While these rules are based on concern for the welfare of the children in their care, many feel that most agencies are unfairly restrictive. Are all people over a certain age too old to meet a child's needs? Are no single people or working mothers able to be good parents to infants? Each family has a right to be evaluated on its own merits, but an agency is often unable to grant that right.

Usually any couple who gets far enough with an agency to be seriously considered for a child must undergo a home study. Just what this involves varies among agencies.

"We were both given complete physicals," said Ellen O'Brien. "Then our home was visited. After that we were required to see a psychologist twice a week for five months. We talked about everything—budgets, child discipline, our goals personally and as a couple, education, relationships with our friends and with our families, our relationship as a couple, how we fight and how we make up—everything! This was not a Christian agency, but they were very interested in how our Christianity affects our everyday lives. That agency knows everything there is to know about us."

Some people greatly resent the home study. They consider many of the subjects Ellen O'Brien mentions to be matters of privacy. But others, like Ellen and Dan, appreciate the questions.

"The counseling we got was fantastic!" Dan O'Brien said. "Ellen and I learned to communicate well with each other. Even if we had never gotten a baby, the counseling would have been worth all the time and tears we spent. As a couple we will never be the same."

The agency with which the O'Briens worked received almost 2,000 applications in one year. Nearly 650 were accepted. Ellen and Dan were one of the 24 families who received babies. That means that there were approximately 1,976 disappointed families at just that one agency in that single year. Brad and Lenore Lombardi were one of the disappointed couples.

"We filled out an application, but the agency wouldn't even interview us," Lenore said with a trace of bitterness. "I called and tried to talk to someone by phone, but the woman who answered would only say, 'I'm sorry, but we do not interview rejections.' I cannot tell you the shock and confusion I felt. My husband and I were both in our early thirties, so surely we were not too old. We had been happily married for seven years. Our lovely, spacious home had a very small mortgage, and other than that we had no debts at all. Brad owns his own construction business, which is very successful, so we could easily support a child. What was wrong with us? We've asked ourselves this question a thousand times." Shaking her head she said softly, "We never did find out."

Brad and Lenore's case is not unusual. Most agencies are very reluctant to discuss their reasons for rejecting a couple. Often the reason is that the agency already has such a long waiting list that it does not feel it is fair to add another name. Sometimes, with there being so few babies available, a family is automatically eliminated from consideration because it already has a child. But since no explanation is given, the family assumes that there is something terribly wrong personally. I hold that every rejected family is entitled to an explanation, no matter what the situation is.

INDEPENDENT ADOPTIONS

An independent adoption is the other option open to families who want to adopt. Independent adoptions are legal in all but a few states (see appendix 1). In these transactions the biological mother does not surrender her baby to be placed at the discretion of someone else. Instead she agrees to put the child in a family whom she herself selects. A mediator, usually a lawyer, gathers all the information he can about several couples who might be suitable parents for this specific baby. He gives the information to the expectant mother. If she has any questions, she can ask them through the mediator.

As a rule, both the birth parents and the adoptive parents wish to remain anonymous. If the families want a face-to-face meeting, that can be arranged. In any event, the final choice of a home and family for the child lies with the biological mother.

"When we got nothing but discouragement from the adoption agency, Brad and I decided to take matters into our own hands," said Lenore Lombardi. "We knew that there were babies who needed homes, and we knew that we would be good parents. I decided to write letters to hundreds of doctors throughout the state telling them all about Brad and me and our great desire to adopt a baby. I even sent along several pictures of us. Any doctors who knew of possible babies for us were asked to contact our lawyer, a specialist in independent adoptions.

"It wasn't long before we began to get replies, some of them very encouraging. We were told that many mothers keep their babies simply because they can't bear to blindly give them up with no idea of the kind of homes into which they would be placed.

"Several possibilities developed over the next few months, but each time something happened. Brad always said, 'When it's the right one, it will all work out. We'll just have to be patient.' He surely was right. Early one morning our lawyer called and said, 'Mrs. Lombardi, I have a girl here who looks enough like you to be your sister. She's interested in you and your husband as possible parents for her baby.' That has to have been the most wonderful day of my entire life!"

The Lombardis were impressed by the genuine concern the young woman showed for her unborn child. "She was Catholic, and it was very important to her that the baby be placed in a Christian home," Lenore said. "She had many questions. How did we feel about infant baptism? What did we think it meant to be a Christian? If the baby should be a girl, what would we teach her about abortion? What methods of discipline would we use?" The list went on and on."

When questions such as these arise, some lawyers suggest that the adults involved meet together to talk them over in person. Neither the Lombardis nor the teenaged girl and her boyfriend wanted to do that. Yet Lenore found it almost impossible to communicate these personal Christian values through a non-Christian lawyer. Her solution was to write a long letter to the girl.

"I can tell how very much you love this baby," Lenore began. "And already I love it, too. I want you to know that this thing that has been such a tragedy in your life is the greatest thing that could possibly have happened for my husband and me. We see your child as a special gift from the Lord." Then, in as much detail as possible, she wrote about Brad and herself— their home, their hobbies, everything she could think of. She did her best to answer every question that the girl had asked as honestly and as fully as she could. In conclusion she wrote, "My husband and I want you to know that from the beginning we will teach our baby to know the Lord as Savior and Friend. Already we are praying that God in His tender love and mercy will bring our child to Himself. And most of all we must all always remember that the One to whom this child really belongs is God."

The girl was satisfied, Lenore said. "We were called as soon as our little son was born. From that moment on, we had all the privileges of any other parents. Three days after his birth Garrett was released from the hospital directly to us. No foster homes, no delays—he was ours!"

A quick placement like this is one of the main advantages of an independent adoption. There is, however, also a negative side. It takes approximately six months for adoption to become final, and the natural parents could change their minds during this time. If that happened, the baby would have to be returned to them. This does not happen often, but it is always a possibility.

Another disadvantage of an independent adoption is the cost. Not only are the adoptive parents responsible for all the birth mother's medical bills—including any unexpected complications such as a Caesarean section—but they also must cover all the attorney's fees. This can easily amount to several thousand dollars.*

There are many qualified couples who would never be

---

*Making extra payments to the birth mother is *never* legal. That is considered baby selling and is a very serious crime.

considered for a child by an adoption agency. Through an independent adoption, however, many of these couples are the proud parents of happy, well-adjusted children.

"No agency would even take an application from us," said Shirley Carson. "They didn't beat around the bush, either. They came right out and said that we were just too old."

Stan Carson was forty-nine and the father of three grown sons by his first wife when he married Shirley. Shirley, forty-five, had a married daughter and one in college. Now, two years later, they wanted a family that they could raise together. From the start they knew that their ages would be against them, but even so they were sure they had a lot to offer a child. They were financially secure and the owners of a beautiful home, and they had a great deal of time and love to invest in a child.

"We had been told about a lawyer who did a lot of independent adoptions, so we made an appointment and flew across the country to see him. In less than a year he found a baby for us. The mother was an unmarried fourteen-year-old who was specifically requesting an older couple. She had been raised in poverty and neglect, so it was important to her that her baby be placed with a family who not only had money, but also had plenty of time and interest to spend on the baby. She selected us, and we became the parents of Leanne, the sweetest baby girl any couple could ever hope for."

"That was fifteen years and two more children ago. Looking back, Stan and I are convinced that our age has really been an advantage. We have certainly been better parents to Leanne and her brother and sister than we ever were to our first families." Laughing, she added, "Us, old? Not at all! Our second family has kept us young."

At the same time, some people are wary of independent adoptions and for good reason. Black market dealings, where children are sold for great amounts of money, have existed for a long time. As the supply of healthy infants decreases, the possibilities for such abuse increases dramatically. The buying and selling of babies is a very serious crime. For this reason adoptive parents are forbidden by law to pay any money to the natural parents for the privilege of adopting their babies. Most lawyers who work with adoptions will charge an hourly rate rather than a flat fee so that it will be abundantly clear that he is acting as an attorney and not as a baby broker.

Because of the legal gray areas here, it is important that you be very careful when selecting a lawyer to act as your intermediary. He must be reputable and trustworthy, someone in whom you have great confidence. But he must also be capable of seeing the entire adoption process through in a way that meets all the legal requirements in every state that is in any way involved with the adoption. If this is not done, the adoptive parents could well be faced with legal problems when the adoption is brought to court to be finalized.

Heather O'Brien is now an active four-year-old with bright red curls and big brown eyes. At seven Garrett Lombardi looks and acts just like his dad. Leanne Carson is a fifteen-year-old high school student who is planning to pursue a career as a social worker. All three were adopted as newborn infants. Here is what their parents have to say as they look back on their experiences with adoption:

"God is indeed sovereign," says Ellen O'Brien. "Had He allowed me to have children the way I wanted to, Dan and I would never have been Heather's parents. Even if by some miracle I were able to conceive and have a baby, Heather would never lose her special place in my heart. She is the one who changed my life."

"How we prayed for our son!" says Lenore Lombardi. "No one could ever have wanted a child more than we did. And I'm sure that there is no child who is more loved. Garrett may have been born to another woman, but God made him for us. We are truly, truly blessed."

Stan and Shirley Carson's feelings are just as strong, but for them there is more to the story. At the time they adopted Leanne, neither of them knew the Lord. Today they attribute their coming into Christian faith to Leanne's entrance into their home.

"It was when we got Leanne that I first became interested in knowing God," Shirley says. "From the very first I realized that she was a special gift from God. There is no other way that we could have gotten such a wonderful, healthy baby—not at our age.

"Neither my first family nor my husband's was a great

success. This time I was determined that we would give our child a firm foundation on which to build her life. So I got involved in a Bible study. It was there that I accepted Christ. Two years and many prayers later, Stan came to know Him too. Then, when Leanne was seven years old, she made the decision to ask Jesus to be her Lord and Savior. Our other two have just recently taken this step. Because of Leanne, our very special gift from heaven, we are truly a chosen family."

"We cannot know everything that God knows," says Brad Lombardi thoughtfully. "If we did, we would always say, 'Go ahead, Lord. Do whatever you want to do; it's fine with me.' My favorite verse is Ephesians 3:20: 'Now glory be to God who by His mighty power at work within us is able to do far more than we would ever dare to ask or even dream of—infinitely beyond our highest prayers, desires, thoughts, or hopes.'

"Even though I cannot know all that God knows, I am satisfied that He does have a master plan with every single one of the details already drawn in."

OPEN FORUM

VICTORIA MEYERS: *Ben and I got our first child two months ago. Before he was placed with us, our son spent an entire month in a foster home. I really resent that lost time. A friend suggested that the next time we adopt we could eliminate the foster home by going through a lawyer instead of an agency. Is this true?*

MR. DONNELLY: *An agency won't place an infant in an adoptive home until the final relinquishment documents have been signed. The reason for this is very simple: they don't want to run the risk of having to remove the child if the mother should change her mind and want the baby back. The completion of these documents takes, on an average, from two to six weeks. Until then the mother has all rights to the baby and the infant is kept in a foster home. In independent adoptions, foster homes aren't used. But adoptive parents who receive their infant immediately after birth must realize that they are running a risk. If the birth mother should change her mind, the adoptive parents have absolutely no legal rights to the child. Fortunately it's not likely to happen, but it is a risk.*

VICTORIA MEYERS: *Why does the final relinquishment take so long?*

MR. DONNELLY: *Just getting the necessary documents prepared takes time. The signed release papers—which in many states must be signed in the presence of a licensed social worker employed by a licensed agency—must be accompanied by a certified copy of the baby's birth certificate. But the most important reason for the delay is that the birth mother must be given time to be certain that she truly does want to give up her baby.*

BEN MEYERS: *Are independent adoptions completely legal and above board?*

MR. DONNELLY: *There are only a few states in which such adoptions aren't legal. The idea that independent adoptions are somehow under-the-table affairs is totally false. In California, for example, there was a recent survey taken of the judges whose specific job it is to hear all the state's adoption cases. When asked if they had ever encountered abuses involving independent adoptions, all the judges answered no. Some adoption workers resent independent adoptions, however, because they see them as unfair competition. In one recent year, one local agency reported that they received six thousand inquiries, yet were able to place only forty-two children. With statistics like that, there certainly seems to be room for everyone!*

QUESTIONS FOR DISCUSSION

1. What are the main differences between an agency adoption and an independent adoption?
2. Under what circumstances would it be preferable to go through an agency?
3. When would an independent adoption be better?

4. Yes, But ... A Realistic Picture

Soon it will be Julia's fifth birthday. Julia wants to celebrate by taking cupcakes to her kindergarten class, but her foster mother says that she will probably be moved to a different home before then. Because she has a major hearing loss, Julia needs more time and special care than this foster mother is able to give.

It's an old story for Julia. This artistic, intelligent little girl with big brown eyes, curly black hair, and a turned-up pug nose has spent her short life shuffled from one foster home to another. What she really needs is a family who will adopt her. But because she is older and handicapped, it is doubtful that this will ever happen.

The great majority of families who express interest in adopting a child want a cuddly, alert infant, or perhaps a cute little toddler. But most of the families who request such babies will have to wait for years to get one. Some never will.

The fact is that there just are not enough healthy, white infants to meet the current demand. Even though the birth rate of illegitimate babies is constantly rising, fewer and fewer of them are available for adoption. The main reason for this is that many unwed mothers are now choosing to keep their infants. This trend, along with the prevalence of birth control, the availability of abortion, and the widespread popularity of adoption, has resulted in a real shortage of adoptable white infants. The babies who do become available are quickly placed in the most ideal adoptive homes, usually with families who have been waiting for years.

The American society is currently in a period of adjusting values. It is too bad that this is occurring only because healthy white babies have become scarce. Today if a family wants a healthy, white infant, they will probably be disappointed. There are, however, many little children already legally freed for adoption who remain in desperate need of permanent homes. Like Julia, they grow up bounced from one foster home to another. Many of them have been waiting for years to find families that will welcome them into their homes and their hearts. Most will wait a lifetime.

Who are these unwanted little ones? They are older, handicapped, racially mixed, or minority children. They are siblings who must be placed together. Like any other children, they come in all shapes and sizes. Some are outgoing and some are shy, some extremely bright and others slow. They come from various ethnic, cultural, and religious backgrounds. Each one has his own unique personality, potential, talents, and limitations. And like any other child, each of these has a driving need to be special and important to someone. He needs a family to care about him, to care for him, and to love him.

A CHANGE IN ATTITUDES

In recent years there has been a major shift in the emphasis of many adoption agencies around the country. Instead of settling for the easy placement of healthy newborns, they have begun to concentrate on finding adoptive homes for the already available but hard-to-place children. In an effort to find families for them, the agencies are becoming more flexible in their requirements.

It is difficult to talk in a general way about adoption policies nationwide because state laws vary. Even within the same local area, policies differ from agency to agency. In 1978 the U.S. Congress finally passed the country's first federal legislation on adoption. This law, called the Adoption Opportunities Act, provides for a National Resource Exchange that lists waiting children and waiting parents with a computerized system that keeps track of children in foster care. To find a group in your area that deals with the adoption of hard-to-place children, write:

National Adoption Informational Exchange
  of the Child Welfare League
67 Irving Place
New York, New York 10003

Again, the first concern of any responsible adoption agency is to insure to the best of its ability that every child it places will be raised in a secure, loving, and nurturing home. But by reviewing requirements, application procedures, and the selection of adoptive parents, many agencies have begun to concentrate more on "screening in" than on screening out prospective families. Only applicants who are considered to be incapable of providing good care and a warm, loving home to a needy child are ruled out by every adoption agency.

In serving hard-to-place children, agencies tend to ease their rules and regulations. Today most are willing to consider each case individually and even to waive some of their requirements when it seems appropriate. Two couples who have benefited from this trend are the Allens and the Powells.

Hindered by a poor credit rating and a modest savings account, Fred and Suzanne Allen had been discouraged from even filling out an application for adoption. But they persisted in their determination to have a child. Two years ago, on the basis of Fred's steady income, the Allens were able to adopt a deaf three-year-old boy.

Under the old requirements, Tony and Joy Powell could never have adopted because they don't own a house. Fortunately the agency with which they worked recognized that the ability to provide a secure home with an atmosphere of love and patient understanding is more important to a child than having parents who are homeowners. Last year the way was cleared for the Powells to adopt a brother and a sister who had been abandoned by their parents.

These changes have brought hope to many families whose applications for adoption would have been quickly turned down a few years ago. As a result, many homes are being enriched by the presence of much-wanted, much-loved children. Working mothers, older couples, lower income families, families with other children, and single persons are being recognized as people who can be excellent parents. Suddenly there are many more potential adoptive families around than anyone had imagined. And somewhere along the way, adoption agencies have made an interesting discovery: some of the qualities that have always been considered essential to the nurture of well-adjusted children are not really all that important after all.

And what about the children? If it has been difficult for a family seeking to adopt, just imagine what it has been like for the children waiting for adoption. To be considered acceptable to the "perfect family," a child also had to be perfect. He had to be completely healthy himself, and he had to have been born of healthy parents. Even children with such minor or correctable defects as crossed eyes or a harelip were considered unadoptable. What a tragedy! The basic needs of a child with a physical, mental, or emotional handicap are just as great as the needs of any other child. And who among us would dare to question God's equal and unconditional love for every single one of these little ones?

As agencies began to try to place formerly unadoptable children, they made another discovery. Many of the couples who had requested a "normal" child responded with love and sensitive understanding to the needs of the hard-to-place children. They came forward, anxious to become parents to these little ones and expressing a readiness to cope with problems of all kinds.

For little Julia, who was mentioned at the beginning of the chapter, there is no happy ending. For many other children there is. The desire to love and provide a home for a very special child occurs in different ways and for different reasons. Probably the most common is the one told by Frank and Helen Smithson, an active couple in their early forties.

"We knew that there was little chance of having a baby placed with us," said Helen. "Our age was against us. And to tell the truth, I'm not at all sure that I have the energy to keep up with an active two-year-old. So for us, adopting an older child really made sense.

"Cindy was eight years old when we adopted her. She immediately became the center of our lives. Being an only child was good for Cindy because she was in such need emotionally. She was like a little sponge, ready to soak up all the love and attention that we could pour on. And how she responded!

"God made us for each other, we know that. What Cindy so desperately needed to receive, Frank and I needed to give."

45

FILLING THE EMPTY PLACE

But difficulties in qualifying for a healthy newborn are by no means the only reason for choosing a hard-to-place child. Jerry Woods and his wife, parents of two healthy boys, chose to adopt from the most unwanted group of all—the mentally retarded.

"My youngest brother, Phillip, suffered from Down's syndrome—often known as Mongolism," Jerry said in a quiet voice. "You can't imagine what a blow it was to our family when he was born. But before long we began to see him for what he really was—a very special gift that God in His great wisdom had entrusted to our family. And that's just how he was treated.

"Phillip died of heart failure two weeks before his seventeenth birthday. We all cried for the empty place he left in our hearts. My brother had that pure joy, that unconditional love and trust that is reserved for the very young and the very innocent. From him we learned the vital lessons of tolerance for all people, however God made them.

"Although no parent would ever want his child to be born with such a handicap, I truly wished that my children could have had the chance to grow up loving, caring for, and learning from their Uncle Phillip.

"When our boys were five and seven, my wife and I read a newspaper account of a Down's syndrome baby who had been deserted at birth. After discussing it with our sons, we decided to inquire about the possibility of adopting that baby.

"As it turned out, that baby wasn't available, but in less than two months we were given Tyler, a sweet brown-haired baby with the same disability. That was seven years ago and I can honestly say that Tyler is every bit as precious to us as Phillip was to me. The agency says that Tyler would have had little chance of ever becoming a part of a family had it not been for us. That may be true, but I don't think they realize how much we have gained. Without a doubt we are a better family because of Tyler."

Dennis and Sue Hardy chose to adopt Nancy, a red-haired, freckle-faced eight-year-old. Nancy suffers from cerebral palsy and is confined to a wheelchair.

"Our natural daughter, Allison, also has cerebral palsy,"

said Sue, "so we knew exactly what was involved in caring for a child with this handicap. We also were keenly aware of just how badly such children need the love and support of a caring family. Because of her disability, Allison has always felt isolated. She attends a special school and has never had playmates in the neighborhood.

"Actually it was Allison who first talked about wanting a sister who was like her. After a few months of such talk, my husband and I began to think seriously about adopting a little girl with C.P. We applied, and within months we were introduced to Nancy. She won our hearts on her first visit. Just one year younger than nine-year-old Allison, she was also confined to a wheelchair. The girls loved each other from the start.

"In many ways Allison and Nancy are just like any other sisters. They play together, laugh together, and cry together. Sometimes they argue and sometimes they pout. But in other ways they are closer than most sisters are. Because they have the same handicap, they depend on each other a great deal. They are each other's only real friend. They help and encourage each other. There's no doubt—as a family of four, we are a resounding success."

Some people have a seemingly limitless capacity to love children and a willingness always to make room for "just one more." God has blessed these special people with the patience, understanding, and acceptance needed to expand and adapt their homes to meet the varied needs of many different little ones. Not many have this God-given gift, but Wes and Peggy Mendez do.

"When the youngest of our five children was ten, our seventeen-year-old said, 'Isn't it time we got some more little kids around here?' That was exactly what I had been thinking!" laughed Peggy, a forty-two-year-old grandmother. "With our oldest daughter married and one of our sons away at college, we had plenty of room.

"I asked the placement agency if they had a child who was in special need. Instead of one they told me about the plight of three children: two brothers, aged four and five, and their seven-year-old sister. They had been living in an overcrowded foster home and were to be moved just as soon as a satisfactory place could be found. Although they were legally available for adoption, such a permanent placement was unlikely because they had to be kept together. That night, after a family discussion, we decided to invite the children to spend the weekend with us. They have been here ever since.

"It would be less than honest to say that the adoption has been problem-free. Of course there have been problems. And there have been adjustments for every one of us. But I know that I'm speaking for the entire family when I say that we don't regret our decision to adopt the children. We gave them the home they needed, and they have repaid us a hundredfold by filling our home with the joyous noise and clutter that only comes from happy children.

"There were two more than we had planned on. But really, three are not so much more trouble than one!"

SOMETIMES IT JUST HAPPENS

For some families, adoption isn't planned. It just seems to happen. That's how it was for Matt and Charlene Dunham.

"With three daughters of our own we were already a good-sized family," said Matt, a middle-aged elementary school-teacher. "My salary is not great, and Charlene has been working part-time ever since the girls were little just to make ends meet. Adopting a child had never entered our minds.

"Then Maggie came to my fifth-grade class. She was a sweet child, and smart, but terribly withdrawn and depressed. Just months before, Maggie's parents and older sister had been killed in an automobile accident. Maggie herself had spent weeks in the hospital. When she was released she went to a foster home because she had no relatives. My heart went out to that sad, silent, lonely little girl.

"When Maggie's foster parents wanted to go away without the children for a weekend, I offered to have Maggie spend the two days with our family. It was amazing to see how perfectly she seemed to fit in. She seemed to belong with us. Before the visit was over, Maggie was laughing and playing like any other ten-year-old.

"After that weekend our family started to talk about the

possibility of adopting Maggie. Before school was over for the year, we had a fourth daughter and Maggie had a family."

Should your family decide to adopt a hard-to-place child, you must realize that he or she does not come with a guarantee. Expect a challenge. That way you won't be caught off guard when difficulties arise.

"Three-quarters of the children we have available are boys over seven," one social worker reported. "Most of them come with emotional scars from abandonment, abuse, and neglect. At first I was hesitant to place special-needs children in adoptive homes because I *knew* there would be problems. I am wiser now. With few exceptions, the parents who chose to adopt these children have found a very special reward for loving and accepting them.

"But we neither need nor want 'do-gooders' or 'rescuers,' " the social worker emphasized. "We just want average families who are happy and secure and want a child or children to share their family life. Families or single parents who feel that they can make the commitment to a child with special needs are now given priority in our adoption agency and in many others as well. We welcome the chance to explore with them whether adoption is right for them and, if so, what child would best fit into their home and lifestyle."

Any adoption gives the adoptive parents the great privilege and the awesome responsibility of becoming the most important people in the entire world to a special little person. At the same time the adopted child becomes special to her new family. As they grow together in love, the parents will find that they are giving a great deal of themselves to their new child. But they must do it willingly and lovingly, appreciating whatever she is able to give in return and demanding no more.

"There was a time when we wanted a healthy, white baby girl," said one woman who is still awaiting word on the application for adoption she and her husband submitted two years ago. "But our ideas have changed. We've grown older and more mature. Today we would have no reservations about adopting a racially mixed child or one with a mild physical or mental handicap."

In the chapters that follow we will take a closer look at some of the options available in adoption today. Maybe you will see your own situation and will be helped and encouraged. Or perhaps you will see a need that you can meet especially well because of the particular circumstances in which God has placed you. Surely Jesus was thinking of children like Cindy and Tyler and Nancy and Julia when He said, "Any of you who welcomes a little child like this because you are mine, is welcoming me and caring for me" (Matthew 18:5).

QUESTIONS FOR DISCUSSION

1. What are the options available in adoption today?
2. We have all heard, read, and seen on television the emotional, inspiring stories of wonderfully successful adoptions of problem children. They usually give us a beginning and a happy ending with a few amusing anecdotes sprinkled in between. How can a family best prepare themselves for the realities of such an adoption?

5. Love Comes in Many Colors

Lisa is an active nine-year-old, the youngest of Gary and Joyce Barber's four children. Like her older brothers, she is on the local swimming team. Like her older sister, she plays violin in the school orchestra. Unlike her brothers and sister, Lisa is adopted.

"When the children were young, they were always being asked why their baby sister didn't look like them," Joyce Barber said. "They would answer, 'She isn't supposed to look like us. She's supposed to look like her!' "

Lisa Barber was one of the thousands of children fathered by American G.I.s in Vietnam. These children were despised by the Vietnamese people because of their mixed race and rejected by the United States government, which refused to take any responsibility for them. So multitudes of them were put into filthy, fly-infested, crowded orphanages in Vietnam. They received minimal care and attention. Hundreds died from malnutrition or commonplace diseases such as the measles. Lisa was one of the fortunate ones who survived.

"Gary and I had always thought that someday we would adopt a child," Joyce said. "When our three children were two, four, and six, we saw a television program sponsored by a Christian organization that depicted the tragic plight of the Vietnamese orphans. It told of one case in which an agency in Vietnam had sixty children eligible and ready for adoption, but before their paperwork could be completed, fifty-two of them had died. We knew immediately what the Lord wanted us to do.

"Because of the great emotional outpouring of concern for these orphans, the agencies had to screen the applicants very carefully. Many would-be parents had not really thought through all the ramifications of such an adoption, and after considering the problems that could lie ahead, many of them changed their minds. Although there were more than twenty couples in our first preadoption session, we were the only ones to complete the procedure and finally, ten months later, to get a baby."

One problem that must be faced by any family considering interracial adoption is the burden of prejudice imposed by our society. The reactions vary greatly, both within the community and within the couple's own family. According to one adoption director, the problem is not a matter of educating the public as a whole as much as fostering a sense of understanding and acceptance in individual neighbors and friends and grandparents.

When a family chooses to adopt across racial lines, a new family is being created in which children of different races or nationalities become brothers and sisters. Since the other children of the family will be very much affected by the adoption, it is only fair to discuss the matter thoroughly with them. Their feelings must be taken into account, for any adoption is a commitment for the entire family. Each member must be determined to make it a success.

These considerations caused no problem for the Barber family. For one thing, they adopted Lisa at a time when there was a nationwide outpouring of concern over the welfare of mixed-race children in Vietnam. Many of Gary and Joyce's friends and neighbors were also discussing the possibility of such an adoption. Then, too, the Barbers' own families were encouraging. Gary's aunt and uncle had adopted three Chinese orphans while they were serving as missionaries in Thailand. Now in their twenties, these Chinese "aunties" are favorites of the Barber children.

"Lisa came from Vietnam on a special plane chartered by a group of adoptive parents," Gary said. "Everyone wanted to come along with us to meet the plane—relatives, neighbors, friends, people from our church—but on the recommendation of the social worker, we went alone. We were determined to keep our first meeting with Lisa a very special, private time just for the three of us.

"When we got to the airport two hours before the flight was due in from Saigon, other couples were already there waiting," Joyce continued. "We were so excited, we just couldn't sit still. We spent the time swapping stories with other 'expectant' parents. We met a heart surgeon and his wife who were adopting a little boy with a congenital heart defect. They had requested him because they felt that they were better equipped to handle a problem like his than most other people.

"When the plane's arrival was announced over the speaker, everyone started to cheer. We all rushed to the window and watched as the plane landed. Then one mother called out, 'Here come the babies!' All around us were cries of greeting, hugs and kisses, cameras flashing, while we waited for what seemed like an eternity. Then finally our name was called.

"I can't begin to describe my feelings when the escort placed that tiny bundle in my arms. Gary and I unwrapped her blanket and examined our new daughter from head to toe. From that moment on, she was our baby.

"We couldn't help but think about the host of possible problems about which we had been warned. We were told that, because of the differences in the temperaments and practices of the two cultures and because of the severe emotional strain, many of these babies become disoriented and upset—some even seriously ill. Many are unable to respond to all the loving they receive. We were also warned about the possibility of physical or mental problems that might not show up until later.

"Lisa's amazingly easy adjustment was a pleasant surprise. We congratulated ourselves on our expert parenting. Our baby never cried at all. But then she never smiled or laughed, either. In fact, she seemed almost totally emotionless. Her little face always wore the same serious expression. Although she was six months old, she couldn't sit alone or roll over. She could hardly even hold her head up. When we held something out to her, she just stared instead of reaching for it. But it had been a long time since I had a six month old and I had forgotten what a baby of that age should be doing. So I didn't worry.

"When I took Lisa for her first checkup, the blow came. The doctor examined her carefully and told me that there was a real possibility that our baby was mentally retarded. I was shocked! But by then Lisa was our daughter just as surely as if she had been born to us, and we would keep her no matter what.

"The first thing Gary and I did was to have a long talk with the Lord. We acknowledged the fact that Lisa was His little girl, only loaned to us. We committed her to His sovereign will and promised to love and care for her whatever her condition.

"Next we planned our strategy. Gary took a month's vacation and we spent hours and hours playing with Lisa, holding her, stimulating her in any way possible. The results were amazing! In three weeks she had caught up to where a six-month-old should be. She was alert, active, sitting well, even starting to crawl. The doctor was astounded at her progress. He said it was nothing short of a miracle. We agree. A miracle is exactly what it was."

Gary and Joyce Barber are good examples of the kind of people who successfully adopt children from a different racial background. They are mature, strong, flexible people. They are able to unconditionally accept a child who is different from themselves. They don't follow the tendency to attribute superior qualities to people who are like them and inferior qualities to anyone who is different. With the decision to adopt a child of a different race they demonstrated a willingness to meet, with God's help, any problems that came along, never letting those problems affect their love and acceptance of their child. Although they certainly realized their child's need for a secure homelife, they did not see themselves primarily as "rescuers," nor were they interested in making a social statement. Instead, they recognized and appreciated their daughter for what she was: a special and satisfying addition to their family.

A family who adopts a child of another race is no longer a single-race family. Both the child and her family will have to contend with whatever stereotypes and racial prejudices exist in their community. Also, by taking the child the family is accepting an obligation to share in her heritage. It is a mistake to try to make the child give up her racial heritage to assimilate that of the family. If the family is not ready to be proud of her for what she is, they have no business adopting her in the first place.

"In her hand-drawn pictures, Lisa had always shown people with big round faces and little round eyes," said Joyce Barber. "Then one day, when she was in kindergarten, Lisa drew a different kind of picture. She started out by drawing the usual big round face, but on this one she put small, almond-shaped eyes. 'That's me!' she announced proudly. For the first time Lisa seemed to see herself as she was, not as she saw us. We want to encourage that individuality and also a real pride in her heritage."

Not all interracial adoptions are as smooth as Lisa's. Like the Barbers, Burt and Carolyn Rhoades were deeply moved by the tragic plight of the Indochinese orphans. They opened their home to four children who had escaped from Vietnam with their mother and an uncle.

"The children have been with us for almost two years now," Burt said, "and believe me, these years haven't been easy. When the children first came to us, they were totally engulfed in fear. They would cringe and cover their heads with their arms at any sudden move. The younger ones have pretty much overcome this fear, but ten-year-old Hoa is still a real problem. At the first sign of any kind of trouble he rounds up his eight-year-old brother and his two sisters, five and four, and hides them in the hall closet. His whole attitude is one of 'us against the world.'

"When you consider his background, Hoa's actions are understandable. In his ten short years he has been through more tragedy and despair than anyone should have to experience in an entire lifetime.

"In Vietnam, Hoa's father was dragged out of his hut and shot by Communist soldiers. In terror, his mother paid her life savings to have the family smuggled out of the country aboard a jam-packed fishing boat. During a violent storm Hoa's uncle and one sister were swept overboard and lost at sea. Two days later the youngest child was born. The rickety fishing boat finally made it to the Philippine Islands, and the family spent a year in a refugee camp there before they were allowed into the United States.

"Just when things were beginning to look up for the family, a deranged man—also a refugee from Vietnam—broke into their apartment and killed their mother while the children looked on in horror. The authorities picked up the four children and placed them in separate foster homes. They didn't see each other again until they were reunited at our house."

Carolyn picked up the story. "The little girls have adjusted beautifully. They are too young to really remember much of what happened. The younger boy isn't a problem, either. He tries awfully hard to fit into the family. But poor Hoa. He sees himself as a survivor, and everyone around him—including us—as the enemy. We want so badly to help him, but where do we begin? At this point we can only trust the Lord."

COPING WITH RACIAL FACTORS

Some people question the wisdom of going outside the United States to adopt children when there are so many needy ones right here in our own country. Although welfare agencies see to it that homeless children have their physical needs met in institutions or foster homes, the children often grow up starved for the love and security that only a caring family can provide. Many of them are minority or biracial children, and while any child raised without a family faces a life of uncertainty, one who discovers that he was rejected for adoption simply because of his racial background can hardly help but be hurt and bitter.

It would be ideal for all children to be placed with families of their own racial or national backgrounds. Unfortunately, that is not always possible. In the United States the pattern of demand for children does not match the racial makeup of those who are available. There are many more white applicants than there are adoptable white babies, and there are not nearly as many adoptive minority applicants as there are minority babies.

Chuck and Sandy Judson live in an area with a large Mexican population. Their two children, now twenty and twenty-two, were adopted as infants.

"When we decided to adopt, many of the available babies and young children were part Mexican," said Sandy. "But very few Mexican families applied to adopt, and because of the ethnic prejudices in our area, few white couples were interested in taking them. Because the child's nationality didn't make any difference to us, we chose children of Mexican descent. Nick was our first child; he was a small, gentle, sensitive boy. Two years later we got Monica, a real fireball. By the time Monica was two, she already ruled the roost. At five she was taller and stronger than her 'big brother.' She played basketball and softball and ran track in high school. With very little effort she got all As and Bs in school. When Monica was growing up, our house was always filled with kids and noise and fun and laughter.

"But it was different for Nick. He was too small to excel in sports, and academics never came easy for him. He was shy and quiet, and while he was always included in whatever Monica and her friends were doing, Nick felt more comfortable on the sidelines. His two great loves were his music—he plays piano, clarinet, and drums—and Buddy, his beautiful Labrador retriever."

"Monica has traveled through her growing-up years relatively problem-free," said Chuck. "Now twenty, she is a university junior majoring in business and is engaged to a seminary student. But things have been much harder for Nick. A lot of the problem, I suppose, was the contrast between him and his athletic, outgoing, popular younger sister—a common situation even among natural-born siblings. But I also think that his adoption by an Anglo family was a contributing factor.

"In our area most Mexicans occupy a pretty low social status. Nick has Latin features, but because of his name and his family, people didn't think of him as being of Mexican descent. Without realizing what they were doing, other kids would make racial slurs or uncomplimentary remarks about Mexicans in his presence. That certainly did nothing to help foster a sense of pride in his own heritage.

"Since his preteen years Nick has had to battle low self-esteem. If I had it to do again, I would make a conscious effort from day one to build up our son's sense of self-worth and to encourage pride in who he is. This is important for any child, but for one who is adopted and physically different from his family, it is especially crucial."

PROTECTION FROM INTOLERANCE

There is much controversy surrounding interracial adoptions. Many people wonder if Caucasian parents can properly prepare a minority child for life in a prejudiced world. There are even those who go so far as to say that minority children should remain under foster care and in institutions rather than be placed in the homes of willing white families. What a tragic point of view!

The sad truth is that in today's American society a child of minority heritage is likely to face prejudice no matter who raises him. But with parents and a loving, understanding, stable Christian home, that child should be able to face life secure in the knowledge that he is truly loved and wanted. Such a foundation is the only real protection any minority child has against intolerance in society. Parents who see themselves and their children not as white or black or brown or any other color, but rather as children created in the image of God, will succeed in making a minority child a part of their family. They can help the child to develop a sense of personal worth and value that will equip him to overcome the problems of life rather than be overcome by them.

JUST A PLAIN KID

It is much easier to adopt transracially if the family lives in a racially mixed community. No child likes to be different. Being the only oriental or black child in a school isn't easy. A child who lives in a community where there are friends, neighbors, teachers, and classmates of his own racial background can be just a plain kid instead of "the adopted black child."

Larry and Janelle Kingman are the parents of two sons by birth and of Katie, a ten-year-old black girl they adopted as a baby. Even though they live in a predominantly white neighborhood, the Kingmans have experienced few problems over race. Katie is a bright girl who is at the top of her class scholastically. She is a natural leader and always has many friends. Only recently has she begun to speak about her hidden conflicts and concerns.

"Once I went to Los Angeles on a field trip with my school class," Katie said thoughtfully. "I saw busses full of kids who looked just like me. I kept wondering if any of them were my real brothers or sisters."

Katie paused, then added, "You know what I really hate? I hate it when people ask me why I'm different from my family. I don't want to be different!"

Katie Kingman's parents have tried to help her come to

terms with these conflicts and develop a true sense of pride in who she is.

"Last year we decided to transfer Katie to a different school," Janelle said. "The school in our neighborhood is all white. The new one, just a few miles away, has a fair percentage of black students. Now, in addition to her neighborhood friends, Katie has black friends with whom she can more easily identify. Also, at the suggestion of her teacher, we are helping Katie with a project that has to do with tracing her roots. It has really been interesting for all of us."

"There is one question that we're asked all the time," Larry interjected. "People always say, 'How would you feel if your sons decided to marry black girls?' Well, Janelle and I have talked about it and I honestly say that it wouldn't matter at all. In fact, our oldest son is now dating a black girl. As for Katie's choice of a lifetime partner—white, black, other minority—it makes no difference to us."

After a pause Larry continued, "I must tell you, though, that we're not really as open-minded as you may think. There is one area in which we are very prejudiced. We would be very distressed if any of our children were to marry a non-Christian."

UNEXPECTED BLESSINGS

The problems, concerns, and considerations of interracial adoptions are certainly greater than those of classic adoptions. Still, every family I interviewed who had been involved in such an adoption emphasized the very special—and often unexpected—blessings that their adopted child had brought to their home.

If you are interested in finding out more about the possibilities for interracial adoption where you live, contact your local adoption agency. Names and addresses of American agencies that specialize in foreign adoptions can be obtained by writing to:

The Children's Bureau of the United States
Department of Health and Human Services
P.O. Box 1182
Washington, D.C. 20013

Ask for the National Directory of Intercountry Adoption Services.

"I feel sorry for the people who tell me how wonderful we are for having adopted Katie," said Janelle Kingman. "It's sad that they can't understand that we are the lucky ones. By giving her to us, God has blessed our family more than I can ever tell."

OPEN FORUM

KEN RANDLE: *Our son is of another nationality, one not held in very high esteem in the area where we live. I think I made a mistake in how I handled him. I was guilty of not being aware of his conflicts and feelings of being different and inferior.*

DR. MCDILL: *If you had it to do again, what would you do differently?*

KEN RANDLE: *I would take my role of fathering more seriously. I would keep in close touch with him and work hard at keeping the lines of communication open. Then I could guide him along and help him to come to terms with who he is.*

DR. MCDILL: *That's important for every parent—especially for fathers, who often fail to realize just how important their parenting role really is.*

QUESTIONS FOR DISCUSSION

1. What were the elements that made the Barbers' adoption of Lisa so much easier than the Rhoades' adoption of the Vietnamese children?
2. What might the Rhoades do to help Hoa adjust?
3. The problem of self-esteem is of concern to many people today. What practical steps would you take to help your child develop a healthy self-esteem? (There is more about this in chapter 12.)

6.   *God's Special*
       Children

Throughout history man has placed great value on physical and mental strength. In primitive times the problem of imperfect babies was usually solved simply and quickly. The child died.

Today in our enlightened age and sophisticated society, imperfect children whose birth parents cannot or will not care for them are usually placed in a system of foster care or institutional living. Only occasionally are they adopted. While many people are moved by feelings of sympathy and pity, not many have an understanding love strong enough to cause them to want to take one of these children as their own.

In the past, children with handicaps were not considered adoptable. It never occurred to social workers that there might be some families who would welcome and value these children in their homes. But times are changing. More and more families are now choosing to lovingly raise children with special needs.

WHY A PROBLEM CHILD?

What motivates families to adopt problem children when healthy children are available? What do they get in return for the extraordinary care and responsibility these children require? Consider Mike and Fran Nelson's experience.

When their church began a ministry at a local home for mentally retarded children, the Nelsons—both teachers—volunteered to help out on a regular basis. It was there that they first met Keith, a tiny four-year-old abandoned by his parents at birth. He had been diagnosed as autistic.

"Keith lived in a strange world of his own," said Fran, a woman in her middle forties. "He didn't show the slightest response to anyone or anything around him. I worked and played with many of the other children, but I just couldn't keep

61

my eyes off that little boy. He sat in silence, playing unknown games with his fingers or gently knocking his head against the wall. I was really intrigued. What could be going on in that little mind of his?

"To the workers at the home Keith was little more than an accessory to the room's furniture. Each morning he was carried in and set down in his corner, and there he stayed until someone carried him to his bed at night. He never talked, he never smiled, and he never cried."

"I really wanted to work with Keith," Mike said, "even though the nurse told me that it would be a waste of time. I couldn't get over the feeling that there was a lot of potential locked up inside him. Maybe we just needed to find the right key. The children with whom Fran and I were assigned to work had very limited mental abilities. The most we could hope for was that they would eventually be able to feed and dress themselves. But with Keith, no one really knew. Anything was possible."

Because of their interest in Keith, Fran and Mike spent more and more time at the home. Whenever possible they would talk to Keith, sing to him, play with him—anything to try to get his attention. But weeks and months passed with no change. The situation seemed hopeless. Keith never gave the slightest indication that he knew or cared that they were there. After six months, the Nelsons—disappointed and discouraged—were ready to admit defeat.

"We were so sure that God was going to accomplish a miraculous healing right before our eyes," Fran admitted. "But it just wasn't happening. We decided that it would be best for everyone if we stayed away from the home for a while.

"Two weeks later we got a telephone call from the nurse at the children's home. She said that Keith seemed to be looking for us! For several days he had been less interested in his finger games and, for the first time in his life, he was looking around. We were back that afternoon."

"After six more disappointing months with Keith," Mike said, "I read an article about two researchers at a university near our home who had developed a very successful program for working with autistic children. I called them and described Keith, and they agreed to see him right away. But when I asked the home for permission to take him to the university, my request was denied. Rules and regulations, you know. I was frustrated and angry! Fran and I had grown to really care about that little guy. We felt as if we were fighting for *our* child!

"After a lot of prayer, discussion, and counsel, Fran and I decided to ask permission to adopt Keith. We had seen his full medical evaluation and report, so we were well aware of the uphill battle we would face. The medical prognosis wasn't good. Still, we were convinced that the Lord had already brought us together in a very special way, and we wanted to be sure that Keith would have every possible opportunity. We wanted him with us.

"The pile of red tape we faced was monumental, but finally Keith was released to our care. Amid dire warnings and reminders that we could always return him before the adoption became final, we took our little son home."

"The program in which Keith was enrolled was a rigid, difficult, sometimes seemingly heartless one," Fran said. "Many, many nights I fell into bed exhausted and cried myself to sleep. Each morning, before even attempting to get out of bed, I prayed, 'Show me just one little victory today and I'll be satisfied.' And that's exactly what God did. It was those little victories that carried us through.

"What a little trooper Keith was! He was the most single-minded, determined little fellow I've ever seen. You might call him just plain stubborn. But it was that trait that kept pushing him on.

"Keith is now nineteen years old. If you're expecting me to say that he has grown into a perfectly normal young man, you'll be disappointed. He hasn't. But when you consider what he was, and what he would have been had he remained in that institution, our son is perfect.

"This year Keith graduated from a vocational high school. The first three rows of the auditorium were filled with friends and relatives who had shared in his long struggle toward this day. When he was handed his diploma, there wasn't a dry eye among us. Our graduation gifts to him were a new watch and— at his request—a construction-worker lunch box to take to work.

"Keith had a job waiting for him on an assembly line, a job

he had found himself. The next month he moved into a house with six other young men with similar disabilities and a live-in couple who act as house parents. He rides the city bus to and from work and anywhere else he wants to go. His Sundays are spent with us."

"We're proud of our son," Mike said. "He's a happy, self-sufficient, Christian young man who is determined to be a contributing member of society. I hate to think of how close he came to spending his life sitting in a corner of that institution, doing nothing but playing with his fingers and hitting his head against the wall. It makes me wonder, how many other children are there out there like Keith?"

There are many. Thousands of the children awaiting homes have physical and mental disabilities. Their problems range from short-term, relatively unimportant disorders to life-threatening illnesses.

WHAT REASONS ARE GOOD ENOUGH?

Any family interested in adopting a special-needs child must consider the matter carefully and prayerfully. Feelings of pity and guilt are not good-enough reasons for such an adoption. Nor is an emotional or romantic idea of the miracles God will perform for that child. It is vitally important to approach the adoption realistically. Sometimes God chooses to work a miracle, but more often He does not. An adoptive family must be prepared to accept His answer either way.

It is one thing to read about a child with a handicap. Living with his problem day after day and year after year is quite another. Well-meaning new parents can easily become overwhelmed by the realities of daily life, by the lack of resources and understanding available, and often by the lack of knowledge on the part of the very professionals on whom they depend for help, guidance, and solutions.

A unique kind of family is needed for such an adoption to be successful. Parents must have extra patience and love for children with special needs. They must find satisfaction in small, slow gains, and they must be able to rejoice in gradual improvements. They must be able to look upon a child like Keith and see what he can accomplish, not what he can't.

The task requires people who can genuinely value such children and appreciate their individual potential. Like Mike and Fran Nelson, the families must emphasize giving to the child rather than receiving from him. They should be able to see something of great value in their child, to accept with pride whatever he can achieve, and to demand no more. After all, not everyone has to become a doctor or a lawyer or a school teacher to be successful. Most of all, these families need a deep faith in God so that they will have His strength and guidance supporting them daily.

Families who decide to adopt children with special needs must be willing to accept the fact that their child will be more dependent on them than is usual. Yet they must also encourage him to become as independent as he possibly can be. It is vitally important that the child never be viewed as a second choice, accepted as the most convenient alternative to what the parents "really wanted." The handicapped child, like any other, has a right to be loved because of his own personal worth as a human being, created in the great wisdom of God.

When Don and Emily Owens adopted Curt they had no intention of choosing a handicapped child. To all appearances their newborn son was perfect in every way. It wasn't until he was six months old that Emily began to suspect that something was wrong. After a special battery of tests Curt was diagnosed as suffering from muscular dystrophy, a degenerative genetic disease for which there is no known cure. His disease was expected to progress to the point where he would need a wheelchair, perhaps even be confined to bed.

"When Curt's condition was discovered, the adoption had not yet been finalized," Emily related. "Everyone—our families, our friends, even our adoption case worker—advised us to return him to the agency and to wait for a healthy child. We prayerfully and painfully considered our options.

"Don pointed out that we had originally wanted to have a child born to us. Had this happened, there's no guarantee that our baby would have been perfect. And then we remembered the months we spent awaiting Curt's arrival. We had specifically prayed, 'Lord, you have a child picked out for us. Make him or her exactly the way You want our baby to be.' Now here Curt was, just the way God had made him, and God doesn't make mistakes. Our answer was obvious. How could we even have considered trading our baby in for a new, improved model?"

"God promised not to give us any job to do without also providing us with the resources necessary to get the job done," Don added. "We determined that we wouldn't stand around wringing our hands saying, 'Why us?' Instead we would press on saying, 'Lord, what now?' God can perform miracles. He *can* heal Curt. This we firmly believe. But we don't demand it. If God says no, if Curt's condition continues to deteriorate, it won't affect our love for him. He is now and he will always be our child."

At ten, Curt Owens is a bright, outgoing, well-adjusted boy. The effects of the disease are relatively mild. Sometimes he must use a wheelchair, but usually he does well on crutches.

"We have pointed out to Curt that most parts of him are like everyone else," added Emily. "He has the ability to love and to be loved, to learn and to accomplish, to know God and to become His child. The characteristics that make him different are the very things that make him special and unique."

Curt had something to say too. "My mother and father really love me. They didn't have to keep me—they wanted to. That's how I know they really love me."

APTITUDES AND LIMITATIONS

Children with handicaps, like all children, have certain aptitudes and limitations. They can achieve in some areas even though they cannot achieve in others. It's important for all parents to encourage their children to develop skills according to their natural abilities. The child with special problems needs guidance from his parents to help him form a realistic view of himself so that he will be able to establish goals that he really can achieve.

It is especially important to match the right adoptive family with the right child when special needs are involved. In some families a child's epilepsy would only be a manageable inconvenience, while in another it would be a constant source of concern and embarrassment. Remember, in adoption you *do* have a choice. Even if you are willing to adopt a child with special needs, it's unrealistic to think that you will feel the same about every handicap. Take a close look at your educational expectations, your lifestyle, your personal prejudices (which we all have), and your family's finances.

A family's financial situation is important in certain special needs. Problems like Curt's and Keith's can cause a financial drain on any family. In many cases governmental subsidies may provide the help the family needs. To make the adoption of hard-to-place children feasible, most states have some programs available (see appendix 1). The amount of the financial aid and the requirements for qualifying vary widely. There is also a new federal tax law that allows parents who adopt children with special needs to deduct up to $1,500 of their expenses, including agency and attorney fees. Because laws can be changed at any time, it is wise to check with your attorney or tax consultant as to the amount of aid to which you may be entitled.

LEARNING BY EXPERIENCE

Foster parents who accept children with special problems on a temporary basis sometimes become so lovingly attached to the children that they want to keep them permanently. These parents have a real advantage. They have already learned how much time and energy a child requires day by day. This was the experience of Bill and Marilyn Schultz.

"We love children and always wanted our own," said Marilyn, a soft-spoken woman of thirty. "When we turned in our application at the adoption agency we were told to expect a wait of several years. To fill the time, and also to prepare ourselves for parenthood, Bill and I decided to become foster parents. Three little ones were placed in our home in the first year. Each of them stayed just long enough for us to get attached to them; then they were taken away. Every time I had to say goodby, I cried for days. Just when I had decided that foster care was not for me, we got the call about Anna.

"Anna had been born to a married couple with four other children, all boys. Her parents had really wanted a girl and they were ecstatic—until they found out about her problem. Anna had been born with an abnormality of the esophagus that caused her to stop breathing several times a day. Her parents, feeling that they were not able to cope with such a deformity, left her at the hospital. The social worker who called us said it was just as well. If Anna's parents had taken her home, it's doubtful whether she would have lived more than a few days.

"Bill and I agreed to take Anna until another home could be found for her. We were taught to care for her, to feed her, and to revive her when she stopped breathing. A warning alarm was attached to her crib, but whenever she was out of her crib she had to be watched constantly.

"The doctor told us that if Anna could be kept alive, she would almost certainly outgrow her condition. But as we soon learned, that was a very big 'if.' That very night she stopped breathing, and we couldn't revive her. We had to call an ambulance. After that we lived constantly on the edge of panic."

"I wasn't in favor of taking Anna," said Bill, a construction worker. "I had seen how brokenhearted Marilyn got each time one of the other kids was taken away. What would happen to her if this baby should die? That was a real possibility, you know. But I finally agreed, and after we had Anna for a few days I found that I was the one who was getting emotionally involved! There's something inexplicably engaging about a baby who literally depends on you for her very breath.

"By the time Anna was six months old she had become a part of us. We knew that we couldn't let her go, so we asked about adopting her. At first her natural parents wouldn't release her, but later they changed their minds and signed the papers.

"Everyone told us that we were foolhardy to adopt a baby who could die at any minute. I guess in a way we were, but we just couldn't stand the thought of Anna being taken away from us. Anyway, we were so used to her condition by then that it hardly seemed abnormal any more."

"Anna is now six years old, a first-grader who would make any mother proud," beamed Marilyn as she passed around a picture of her brown-haired, green-eyed daughter with deep dimples and no front teeth. "It's been over a year since she's had a serious breathing attack, although we still have to watch her when she eats. She's scheduled for surgery on her esophagus, and the doctor says that afterward her problem will be a thing of the past. Anna will be as normal and as healthy as any other little girl."

"I'm really glad that we weren't given one of those perfect babies," added Bill emphatically. "They all got good homes. But our Anna probably wouldn't even be alive today without us."

Simply loving and accepting a special child into your home is not enough, however. Parents must also instill in the child a sense of identity and self-worth. Most children with handicaps are convinced that they were given up by their mothers because they were not good enough. In some cases, like Anna's, that is true. In any case the child must be told and reassured that she, like every other human being on earth, was created in the image of God. God does not call us to understand His reasons for everything He does. He instructs us to trust in His perfect wisdom.

The really fortunate families of special children have neighbors, friends, and relatives who are warm and understanding toward their children. These people are ready to open their hearts to them and to judge them only for the values they have, not for the skills they lack. But some people are shy, uncertain, and embarrassed in the presence of such children; they must learn to become comfortable with them. Occasionally there are those who never will be able to accept them; it may help to remember that they—not the child or his parents—are the real losers. It is essential that parents help their children to deal with the possibility of rejection.

HELP FROM OUTSIDE

Prejudice and rejection, added to the difficulties caused by the handicap itself, take their toll on both the adoptive parents and the child. Sooner or later the time comes when outside help, comfort, and encouragement are needed. A valuable source of supportive help can be found in other parents who have gone through, or are now experiencing, the same problem. Others who can help are psychiatrists, psychologists, pastors, and social workers. If you find it necessary to search out support people, don't ever consider it a sign of weakness. It isn't. You are simply showing a mature realization that none of us is meant to exist alone. We need each other.

An important consideration that is often overlooked is the need for relaxation and time alone for the parents of special-needs children. A good arrangement is to find a friend or relative who is willing to assume responsibility for the child while his parents are away.

"For over a year we never let Anna out of our sight," said Marilyn. "Then one Sunday an acquaintance at church, a registered nurse, asked if she could watch Anna for us one day a month so that we could have a little time to ourselves. We reluctantly agreed. The first time, we stayed away barely two hours and worried the whole time. But the next time was easier and we stayed away a little longer. Soon we were taking the whole day and enjoying every minute of it. We even found that we enjoyed Anna more after our monthly breaks."

Some people think that taking time away from their child means they aren't good parents. This just isn't true. What it does mean is that those parents are human and have a normal human need for rest and relaxation.

The most important of all considerations for the family thinking about adopting a child with special needs is the child herself. She is the one who so badly needs to love and to be loved. Whatever the problem, it will almost certainly make some aspects of her life more difficult for her and for her adoptive family. But it does not affect who she is.

Can you give the time, the care, the patience, and the understanding it takes to raise a child with a handicap? For those whom God calls on to raise His special children, there are great satisfactions and rewards, although not necessarily our traditionally accepted ones. But who's to say that our traditional values are true in this case? Perhaps our values would be much different if we could see through the truly wise, loving eyes of the Creator. God says, "For I know the plans I have for you. . . . They are plans for good and not for evil, to give you a future and a hope" (Jeremiah 29:11).

QUESTIONS FOR DISCUSSION

1. What are the important qualifications for adopting a special-needs child? Which ones do or do not fit your situation?

2. Again it must be emphasized: in adoption there are no guarantees. This is especially true when children with handicaps are involved. The Nelsons, the Owenses, and the Schultzes could just as well have seen their children's conditions degenerate instead of improve. Do you think they were prepared for this possibility?

7.   *No Longer Babies*

"Even before we were married, Gordon and I agreed on the type of family we wanted," said Janet Van Dyke, an elegant woman of thirty-five. "We wanted children, but we did not want babies.

"Again and again my mother complained that I was denying her the pleasures of having a grandbaby of her own. According to her, I was just too selfish to let a baby interfere with my career.

"I'll admit that my job as purchasing manager for a large department store was—and is—a very important part of my life, but that wasn't my reason for not wanting to have a baby. It's just that I never was baby-oriented. Both Gordon and I felt that we would be better parents to an older child.

"When we took our request for a school-age child to the county adoption agency, we were welcomed enthusiastically. Any child over the age of four, it seems, is considered a geriatric loser in adoption circles. Still, the social worker to whom we were assigned wanted to be very sure that we knew exactly what we would be getting into. She covered the potential problems so thoroughly that we began to suspect that she might actually be trying to scare us off. Again and again she reminded us that many, many adjustments would be necessary."

The social worker was right. An adoption involving an older child entails many adjustments for both the parents and the child. In many ways the arrangement is more like a marriage than an adoption. There must be a spirit of acceptance on both sides and a genuine willingness to give as well as to take. For this kind of adoption to be successful, both the child and the new parents must agree to live together as a family, and both sides must be willing to make concessions for the sake of harmony.

Since he comes with his personality already formed, an

older child will not easily be molded into the likeness of his new parents. He comes with a past, with his own memories and established tastes, with his own pattern of life. Older children have usually been in foster care for several years and have been shifted from home to home. They have learned how risky it is to trust, how dangerous to love. Some have suffered physical and emotional damage.

It takes time for love to grow between the adopted child and his new parents. Though the child desperately wants to be a part of a loving family, he may act in ways that serve only to drive others away. There will be moments when you will wonder how you ever got yourself into this relationship, and there will be moments when you will wonder why you waited so long. In between there will be challenges, victories, and some losses.

"Six months after we were approved as adoptive parents," Janet related, "Eric, a seven-year-old blond with huge brown eyes and freckles on his nose, came to visit our home. He and his ten-year-old brother Craig had been living with a couple who were in the process of adopting them. But when that couple filed for divorce, the brothers were returned to the agency. It was decided that the boys' only hope of ever being adopted was to split them up and make them available to separate families.

"When Eric arrived to stay with us, I took a six-month leave of absence from my job. I thought that by spending time together we could really get to know each other. But Eric was a quiet, withdrawn boy who seldom spoke. When he did talk, it was always about the good times he had had in his foster homes and how much he missed his brother. I knew for a fact that Craig had bullied Eric unmercifully, but to hear the boy talk you would have thought his brother had been a saint. I began to wonder if Eric would ever love and accept Gordon and me as his family."

Though confusing and frustrating to his new parents, Eric's reactions were completely normal. He was experiencing a deep sense of separation, and he needed time to grieve over his loss. Fortunately his new parents were ready and able to give him the support he needed to resolve his feelings of sorrow and conflicting loyalties.

"Gordon was very good to Eric during this difficult time,"

Janet continued. "He spent hours with him and in very special ways demonstrated that he truly valued him for who he was—a good boy, worthy of our love. Gordon felt that Eric must understand that he was in no way responsible for anything that had happened in the past. My husband's excellent fathering deserves a great deal of credit for our son's relatively easy adjustment.

"That's not to say that the adoption was problem-free. Eric went through a time of testing us, but we dealt with his misbehavior immediately and firmly. We made it perfectly clear that we expected him to make an effort to adjust, but we also let him know that we were willing to do the same. In the end we were able to reach a happy medium and come to a mutual understanding. Eric was accepted for who he was; we did not try to make him over to be like us. In really important areas we were definite and strict, but in areas that didn't matter so much we were relaxed and flexible. It wasn't long before Eric developed a true appreciation for his new home and a real love for us. Never once did he say that he wanted to leave."

Three years after Eric's adoption, Gordon Van Dyke was killed in an automobile accident. His death was a terrible blow to the little boy who had spent his whole life struggling for security and a sense of permanence.

"Gordon's tragic death was the most terrible thing that has ever happened to me," Janet said. "But it was even worse for Eric. He and his father had become extremely close. At first Eric was angry. He felt that his father had deserted him just as everyone else had done before. But that anger soon gave way to overwhelming sadness. Through our shared sorrow Eric and I were drawn closer to each other. The morning after Gordon's funeral Eric came and climbed into bed with me. With tears in his eyes he said, 'We'll stick together, Mom. You take care of me and I'll take care of you.'

"Soon after Gordon's death, Eric's insecurities began to resurface. Even though he was ten years old, he did not want me out of his sight. Everywhere I went, he went. He even took to sleeping in a sleeping bag on my bedroom floor. After three months of this, a business situation came up which called for me to be out of town for a weekend. I considered taking Eric along, but it just wasn't practical. When Gordon's sister offered to keep him, I agreed. It was awfully hard on Eric, but it was just what he needed. He had to learn that I could go away and always be depended upon to come back. Gradually he began to get over his terror of losing me.

"Gordon's relatives and my own here in town have been a great help. My sister-in-law and her husband have a boy just older and a girl just younger than Eric, and they all get along together very well. Even my parents, who at first were so opposed to the adoption, have grown to love Eric. He and my dad have developed an especially close relationship.

"Eric is very open about his adoption," Janet continued. "Most of his questions concern Gordon's and my national background and our family histories. Everything he hears from me and his other relatives is incorporated into himself, and it all becomes a part of who he is.

"So far Eric has shown almost no interest in his birth family, though his history would be quite easy to trace. His brother Craig remembers a lot and has many of the family's records. When Eric came to us, he brought a book containing his baby pictures, pictures of his mother and brother, and pictures of his different foster families. He enjoys having me add to the book. The other day he asked me to put my picture on top of the picture of his birth mother. When I asked him why, he said, 'Because I don't even know that woman. You're my real mother.' "

Eric's relatively painless adjustment is a testimony to his parents' patient acceptance and sensitive handling, especially the excellent fathering he received from Gordon. The Van Dykes possessed those characteristics important for a couple interested in adopting an older child. They were warm, mature, flexible, understanding, and accepting.

ARE YOU READY?

Families who are considering such an adoption should ask themselves these questions:

- Can we open our arms to a child who, because of his unhappy experiences, may not be able to reach out to us?

- Can we accept the fact that the child has a past of which we will never really be a part?
- Will our new child receive our highest priority?
- Can we accept the whirlwind of activity that the child may bring to our home?
- If it is needed, are we willing to ask for and heed professional counsel?
- Can we accept the possibility that it may take time to gain the child's love?
- Can we be flexible in our lives and our expectations?

Flexibility is probably the most important characteristic of all. No matter how smooth the adoption, one thing is certain: there will be a drastic change in the household. The new parents had better be ready for it.

Ted and Jean Howard approached the adoption agency specifically asking for an older boy.

"My father was born in Georgia," Jean said in a soft Southern drawl. "He lived in an orphanage until he was adopted by a farm couple at the age of ten. I remember hearing him tell about how the farmer came to the orphanage and looked all the older boys over. He tested their strength and asked endless questions about their behavior. Since my dad was large for his age and was quiet and cooperative, he was chosen.

"But it wasn't a son that the farmer and his wife wanted. It was a farm hand: cheap labor. They provided Dad with food and clothes, but love and affection were never included in their business deal. After Dad left the farm at the age of twenty-two, he never saw his 'parents' again. When they died, in accordance with their will the farm went to an uncle.

"Dad never expressed any bitterness or resentment toward the couple. He seemed to accept the adoption as a legitimate business deal that provided him with a better life than he would have had in the orphanage. Perhaps he's right, but it's always bothered me.

"I was amazed when I found out that my father-in-law had been raised in a similar situation. Early in our marriage, Ted and I decided that someday we too would make room for a homeless boy in our family. But our boy would not be raised like his grandfather was. He would be loved. He would be a real son.

76

"When our own children were twelve and nine, we adopted Christopher, an eleven-year-old who had spent his life in a series of foster homes—twelve in two years! Like my own father he was big for his age, being several inches taller than his new older brother. He was a troubled, insecure boy. What Chris had seen and endured in his short life we can only guess.

"Chris's reputation as a troublemaker preceded him, but I had always believed that enough love could win over any child, no matter what his problems. Our first several weeks together certainly seemed to prove my point. Chris was polite, helpful, cooperative, and responsive—everything we could hope for. Then one night, after Chris had been in our home for six weeks, Ted reprimanded him for teasing the dog. To our utter amazement, he completely blew up. He stomped his feet and threw things, slammed doors, and cursed. Then, looking straight at Ted, he yelled, 'You're not my real father! You can't tell me what to do!' I couldn't believe what was happening. How could my motherly love have failed so miserably?"

Christopher was not turning into a juvenile delinquent, and the Howards were not the failures they thought they were. They were experiencing the end of what is often called the "honeymoon period." For six weeks Chris had been on his best behavior, as had Ted and Jean and their natural children. But such a guarded life is artificial, and in time it has to come to an end.

"It was obviously time for me to take action," said Ted, a six-four, former college linebacker. "I decided that if Chris was to be a member of our family, he must be treated like one. I told him to go up to his room. When he refused to obey me, I picked him up and carried him out. Later on, when he had calmed down, we talked about his behavior and agreed on a punishment: the next afternoon he was to clean up the patio. The job was completed without complaint."

Ted was wise to deal immediately and firmly—while not being overly strict—with Christopher's misbehavior. Chris continued to defy and test his father's authority, but Ted had been warned that this would happen, and he was prepared. Armed with resilience, determination, and plenty of energy, he pressed on without compromise throughout the entire period of adjustment.

"I understood Chris's need to test and retest me," Ted explained, "but in order for our home to be a pleasant and secure place for all of us, he needed to adjust—and he needed to do it quickly. My plan of attack was to set firm and consistent limits for him just as I did for my other kids. My end goal was for him to learn to set those controls for himself. This was the first time that Chris had ever had consistent discipline, but I knew that if Jean and I were to be his parents he would have to learn what we expected of our children. We didn't expect overnight success. Short-term goals, for Chris and for us, were enough of a challenge at first. We had to prove to him that when we made a deal, we could be depended upon to hold up our end."

No matter how much an older child is loved and wanted by his adoptive family, there will certainly be some rough times. The child is struggling to make a big adjustment. Bed-wetting, offensive language, lying, stealing, whining, tantrums, and disruptive behavior are common. Some children demand expensive clothes and more spending money as proof of their parents' love. Some will criticize and rebel against their new parents' way of doing things. Some will try to divide the family by setting one parent against the other. Just how long this difficult period lasts depends a lot on the child's age, his personality, his past experiences, and to some extent on his adoptive parents. When he finally reaches the place where he truly feels secure in his parents' love and acceptance, the testing will come to an end.

"We endured six months of Chris's awful behavior," said Jean with a sigh. "The strain was evident in our family. But we were certain that we were doing the right thing and were determined to make the adoption work; not in our own strength—that was long gone—but in the strength of the Lord.

"The hardest thing to accept was that all the love and attention I showered on Chris seemed wasted. He just didn't love me back. I couldn't figure out what I was doing wrong. At the suggestion of our counselor, Ted and I joined a support group made up of five other couples who had also adopted older children.

"We gained an entirely different perspective through that group. We discovered that our problems with Chris were not unique. Everyone there had gone through the same thing. We were encouraged to try to see things from Chris's point of view. As for his loving us, he simply wasn't ready to make himself vulnerable to another new set of parents who, he felt, probably wouldn't keep him anyway. He had been hurt and rejected so many times that he wasn't about to let himself be hurt again. It was up to Ted and me to prove ourselves to him. We had to love him and love him and love him some more, even though we received little in return.

"Do you know what? It really worked! As Chris was consistently cared for, understood, and loved by us, he gradually began to love and trust us in return. His trying behavior was his way of asking, 'Will you love me even if I act terrible?' While we certainly could not condone his behavior, we needed to be flexible and willing and able to cope with it. We had to be sensitive to Christopher's emotional needs, to try to understand why he did what he did. We talked to him about his attitudes, his feelings, his fears, and his expectations. And we shared our ideas with him."

KEEPING THEM TOGETHER

With older children so hard to place, imagine the problems an agency encounters in attempting to find homes for siblings who must be kept together. For most of them, the venture is doomed from the start.

"If people had ever suggested that my husband and I would adopt four kids at once, I would have said they were crazy!" laughed Paula Moreno, a jovial woman of forty-five. "Our home is licensed for foster care. One day a social worker called and begged me to take some kids for a couple of days. I figured, why not? Even in our tiny house we could make do for that short a time. About an hour later the dirtiest and most bedraggled, forlorn-looking little things I've ever seen were herded into our living room. Tony, the senior member of the group, was ten. Scott was seven and the twins, Jenny and Jill, were four. What a motley bunch they were!

"Abandoned by their mother, their alcoholic father had left these little ones pretty much to their own devices for close to three years. The kids' predicament was discovered when the boys were picked up for starting a fire in a vacant lot.

"Fortunately my husband Alex and I have an easygoing household. I don't get upset about too much. The kids didn't feel too threatened here. Alex fell in love with them immediately, and they were his kids from the start. For me it was harder. You can imagine how my workload increased! To be honest, there were days when I would have gladly let them go.

"The kids had never been in a foster home before," Paula continued. "They came to us thinking that they'd be our children forever. Jenny and Jill called us 'Mommy' and 'Daddy' from the first day. Weeks passed, then months, and still the kids stayed on. There just was no place for them to go. Very few foster homes are set up to take in four kids at once.

"Tony, the oldest, was surprisingly mature and responsible. He and Alex became very close. And the twins and I took to each other right away. I was the only mother those little girls had ever known. Scott was our problem. As the middle child he easily got lost in the crowd, except when he was in trouble. Maybe that's why he always seemed to be in trouble. We were willing to work at our relationship, though, and to allow for differences. Alex and I both began to concentrate our efforts on Scott, and gradually he began to come around.

"The relationships among the kids were really perplexing to me. They alternated between defending and protecting each other, and teasing and tattling on each other. They actually seemed to enjoy getting each other punished. Jenny and Jill, those sweet little girls, were the worst of all."

"I could see what they were doing," interjected Alex Moreno. "Each one was trying to prove that he or she was our favorite child. They loved each other, but each one seemed to have an insatiable need to be loved the most. Paula and I refused to play that game. We were determined to love them all the same. And that included Scott."

"By the time the children had been with us for three years," Paula said, "we all felt that we truly belonged together. The big adjustments had been made and we were like a real family. Then it suddenly occurred to me, what if the kids were to be taken away from us someday? Alex and I decided that the logical solution would be for us to adopt them. We asked the kids, and every one of them was in favor of it. In fact, Jenny and Jill thought they already *were* adopted. Next I wrote a letter to their father; he responded that we were right: the children should be with us. The only problem was the mother whom the kids had not seen since she deserted the family six years before. She didn't want them back; she just didn't want them to be adopted. She even showed up in court to protest. But the kids didn't even recognize her, and the judge ruled in our favor."

"From the very beginning we were warned that we couldn't expect to remold the personalities of children as old as ours," Alex said. "We didn't even try. But we did teach them, by our words and even more importantly by our actions. The kids have been with us for seven years now, and all of them have changed radically in their personalities as well as in their general views of life. That includes seventeen-year-old Tony, who came to us half-grown. It also includes Scott, who endured many emotional problems. Why the great change? I'm convinced that it's due to the Lord's working in their lives. What a testimony to the power of God! He can change anyone or anything, even the personality of a troubled child."

"It's hard to believe that there was a time when Tony, Scott, Jenny and Jill were strangers to us and that things happened before I even knew them," said Paula Moreno. "It's hard to believe that I once wondered if we would ever be able to really love each other. It's hard to believe that there was ever a time when we weren't a family." Grinning, she added, "I'm so glad those days are gone."

OPEN FORUM

PAUL CONWAY: *If there's one thing I can't stand, it's dishonesty. But no matter what Margaret and I do, we can't seem to break our daughter of lying and stealing. She was seven when we adopted her and now, two years later, she's as bad as ever.*

PAMELA FRIEDMAN: *That surely sounds familiar. Our son, adopted at the age of six, was just the same. The support group we belong to was a real help. Lying isn't unusual behavior, you know.*

PAUL CONWAY: *But what can we do?*

PAMELA FRIEDMAN: *First of all, it helps to understand why she is doing it. She has probably never learned to trust adults. Some kids will try to lie their way out of everything to keep from getting into trouble. This lying can become an automatic response, especially when the child figures that if you punish her it means you are rejecting her.*

MARGARET CONWAY: *Sometimes it seems as if our daughter actually tries to get herself into trouble. Whatever happens, she seems to try to work it around so that she will end up being the "victim."*

CLIFF FRIEDMAN: *Maybe she has learned that the only way to get attention is to get into trouble. After all, negative attention is better than no attention at all. We had to make a real concentrated effort to give our son lots of positive attention. It took a lot of time, but it really did help.*

PAMELA FRIEDMAN: *These older kids usually come to us with well-entrenched problems and responses. Over and over our support group stressed the importance of consistency, firm guidelines and much praise and support.*

QUESTIONS FOR DISCUSSION

1. According to Janet Van Dyke, her husband Gordon was the one most responsible for Eric's relatively easy adjustment. What do you consider to be the father's role in parenting? How important is it?

2. Jean and Ted Howard spoke of the great help they received from the support group. This idea was emphasized by the Friedmans in the open forum. In what ways can such a group be helpful? How can a person locate such a group? (See chapter 12.)

8.   *Sometimes Parents*

When Stacy and Christine's mother suffered a nervous breakdown, their father found that he could not take care of his young daughters alone. The girls were placed in a foster home until their mother was well enough to care for them again. . . .

Two-year-old Joseph was found sitting on the courthouse steps. Pinned to his shirt was a note that read, "Please take care of Joseph. I have no money to buy him food or clothes, and no place to live." Joseph, too, was placed under foster care. If his mother did not return within one year, he would be considered abandoned and would be free for adoption. . . .

Mary Beth was born without a left arm or foot. Her mother could not accept a child with such a severe handicap, and early the next morning she walked out of the hospital, leaving her newborn daughter behind. Mary Beth was placed in a foster home to await adoption. . . .

Bobby's mother is a drug addict, and his father is in prison. As a baby, Bobby was left alone for hours at a time. He was two years old when concerned neighbors finally called the police. The neglected little boy was taken to a foster home. Bobby has spent six years in foster care. During this time his mother has visited him only five times. Though still on drugs and unable to care for her son, she adamantly refuses to release him for adoption. . . .

. . . Stacy and Christine's mother made a rapid recovery. After spending less than two months in foster care, the girls were able to return home.

. . . Joseph's mother never came back to claim her son, and he has now been legally freed for adoption. But three years have passed and, at the age of five, Joseph is considered a hard-to-place older child.

. . . Although Mary Beth has adapted well to her artificial

83

limbs, her chances for adoption are even lower than Joseph's. Few families want a handicapped child.

. . . Mary Beth and Joseph will probably join Bobby and the hundreds of thousands of other children for whom foster care has become a way of life—the children often referred to as "orphans of the living."

A STATE OF LIMBO

Social agencies generally agree that foster care should be a temporary situation during which permanent plans are made for children. It is hoped that they can return home or, if this is not possible, they can be adopted. In reality, however, foster care is temporary for less than a third of the children who come under the system. For some, there is just no adoptive family available, especially for a handicapped child like Mary Beth or an older child like Joseph. In a case like Bobby's, where the child's parents show even a passing interest in him or flatly refuse to release him, there can be no adoption. Such children will remain locked into this "temporary" state of limbo until they are grown.

It is a sad fact that there are not enough good foster homes for all the children who need them. In many places, out of pure desperation, the screening process for foster families is minimal. The demand is so great that agencies are often willing to look the other way in questionable home situations.

"Even though our home is small and is licensed for only one child," Marie Kauffman said, "it's not unusual for a caseworker to plead with us to take two, three, or even four children 'just for a little while.' They know it's not the best arrangement, but the children have to go somewhere."

Marie Kauffman and her husband Joe—a custodian at an elementary school—are in their mid-fifties. They have cared for foster children for more than twenty years.

"When our own children were little, Joe just wasn't earning enough money for us to live on," Marie said. "I didn't want to go out and get a job, because I needed to be home with the children. Anyway, being a homemaker and mother were all I knew how to do. Our solution was to take in a foster child. Not only did it give us a little extra income, but the child had a chance to live in a loving Christian home.

"I can't even count all the children we've had since that first little girl arrived twenty-three years ago. There have been newborn babies, teenage runaways, handicapped children, even a little three-year-old boy who had a heart attack and died in my arms. One time we had three mentally retarded teenage girls who were in some kind of job training together. We almost didn't take them, but I'm so glad we did. They were a real inspiration to us.

"Some of our children left our home because they were adopted. Some went back to their parents. Some reached that magic age of eighteen, and they graduated from foster care. Some were moved on to other foster homes.

"The very first day a child comes into our home," Marie continued, "we start a special book for him. In addition to medical records and school papers, I write down anecdotes about him: his cute sayings and funny experiences. Joe takes pictures—lots and lots of them. When the child leaves us, we give him the book to keep. We hope that these books help to give some sort of continuity to the children's lives."

"Before any of our children leave our home," interjected Joe Kauffman, "Marie and I take him aside—away from the other kids—and pray with him about the new place to which he'll be going, whether it's back home to his parents or to an adoptive home or wherever. I think this has really helped the children. Not long ago a lady who had adopted one of our little ones called Marie to say thank you. She said, 'I'm not sure what you did to prepare her, but our daughter has had an unbelievably easy adjustment.' Marie told her she wasn't surprised: The Lord has simply answered our prayers.

"To my way of thinking, Marie and I are missionaries as much as anything else," Joe continued thoughtfully. "Most of these children come from very sad situations. They have never had any kind of security in their lives at all. In our home, even if it's only for a short time, they have a chance to be part of a solid, secure Christian family. We take them to Sunday school and to church. They participate in our family's regular Bible reading and prayer times. A lot of these kids have come to know the Lord while they were here."

"Never once have we said no when we were asked to take a child," Marie said. "Joe and I feel that the Lord brings to us those children who can best benefit from our home. This is what the Lord has called us to do: provide a Christian refuge for homeless children."

The Kauffmans' home might be considered an ideal foster home. But even in the best of foster homes a child knows that she does not really belong. Her foster parents may love her and treat her kindly, but they are not truly her parents and she knows it. There is no assurance that she will still be with them next year, or even next week. There is no permanence, no commitment in the relationship.

Children are fed and sheltered in foster homes, but food and shelter alone aren't enough. All children have basic needs that must be met for them to grow into healthy, well-adjusted, productive adults. Family loving is crucial in these early years when the child's personality is being formed. If she is not consistently loved, she does not learn how to love—not even to love herself. Above all, the child must belong to someone she can depend on and trust, someone she knows will not leave her. Children without parents of their own enter life with a serious handicap. Most suffer emotional damage. Few ever achieve their full potential. But there is little else to offer these children. For most, foster care is the best option available.

FROM TEMPORARY TO PERMANENT

Sometimes foster parents become so deeply attached to the children in their care that they want to adopt them. Today, if the child has been freed for adoption, many agencies are making it possible for that to happen. Ned and Beth Simon, biological parents of two daughters, have adopted two of their foster children.

"Neither Tamara nor Jonathan had been released for adoption when they were placed in our home," Beth said. "Jonathan was one of our very first children. He came to us as a terrified, tearful, tantrum-prone baby. Our social worker told us that he had been removed from his home because his mother had abused him so badly. By the time he had been with us for a year he had developed into a fun-loving, emotionally healthy first-grader. We were astounded at the change in him.

"During that entire first year, Jonathan never once heard from his mother, not even on his birthday or at Christmas. But still she refused to release him for adoption. Unless his mother could be persuaded to relinquish her parental rights, or unless those rights were taken away from her by court order, Jonathan was doomed to grow up under foster care.

"During the next two years we became more and more attached to Jonathan, and he to us. Finally one day his mother did drop by—totally unannounced, of course—but he flatly refused to see her. He hid under his bed the entire time she was here. After she left, Jonathan emerged from his refuge and announced, 'I don't want that woman to come to my house anymore. She just wants to hit me!'

"We talked the situation over with Jonathan's caseworker. She encouraged us to go to court, charging his mother with abandonment, to get Jonathan legally freed for adoption. We did. His mother didn't even take the trouble to appear. One year later, Jonathan was ours.

"Tamara was three years old when she was brought to us. She had been found wandering alone on a rainy night and dressed only in her underwear. Her mother had not been home for two days. At first Tamara's mother came to visit quite often. She really seemed to care about that little girl. She told us that she was only fourteen when her baby was born and that she had felt pressured into keeping her. 'But how can I raise a kid?' she asked us. 'Look at me! I'm just a kid myself!' Through tears, she literally begged us to adopt Tamara and give her a good home. 'Maybe then she'll have a chance for a decent life,' she said. The mother never came to visit again."

"Both Beth and I wanted to adopt Tamara," Ned Simon said, "but I was concerned about our finances. I'm a carpenter by trade, and there are times when I can't get much work. We already had three children, and if we were to adopt Tamara, we would lose not only the money we received monthly for her support, but also the medical coverage that was paying for her costly allergy treatments. I didn't want money to stand in the way of her adoption, but for everyone's sake I felt that I had to be practical."

"I could certainly understand Ned's concern," Beth said, "but I felt that if the adoption were the Lord's will, He would surely work out the financial details. Still, I didn't want to push. If it were the thing to do, it would have to come from Ned.

"One evening when the kids were all sleeping, Ned surprised me by suddenly saying, 'Let's go through with Tamara's adoption. She belongs here with us. We'll just have to trust God to provide.' Well, we did go through with it and God did provide. Through a program called Aid to Adoptive Parents, the county offered to continue to pay for Tamara's support until she is eighteen. We had never even heard of this program before the social worker suggested it to us. If that isn't proof of the Lord's leading, I don't know what is!"

"For us, foster care seems to be the first step toward adoption," Ned laughed. "And do you know what? We have just accepted another foster child."

Anne and Bruce Riley are also foster parents, but unlike the children placed with the Simons and the Kauffmans, their little ones are all newborn. The Rileys care for infants from birth until they are legally relinquished by their birth mothers and are placed in adoptive homes. This process can take anywhere from two weeks to two months.

"We have had fourteen foster babies so far," said Anne, a thirty-two-year-old mother of three little girls. "Since they are here for such a short time, we really don't have time to get too attached to them. But it's amazing how different each baby is! From the very beginning they have their own individual personalities. Some are a lot harder to give up than others.

"We often hear complaints about the impersonal, disinterested care babies receive in foster homes. But that just isn't true, at least not in our home. Each baby gets a lot of personal attention and a lot of holding and cuddling from both Bruce and me. No bottle is ever propped up on a pillow for our babies. We try to treat each little one with as much loving care as we do our own girls.

"Mickey was our most recent baby," Anne continued. "Though we had him less than two weeks, we will never forget him. You see, Mickey was adopted by our best friends. It was a providential placement from the very beginning. Mickey's teenage, unmarried mother was a Christian, and she specifically requested Christian parents for her child. She wrote a really neat letter in which she stated her definition of a born-again Christian. It was read to the entire board of the adoption agency. What a witness!

"When our friends saw Mickey at our house, it was love at first sight. For five years their name had been on the adoption agency's waiting list, and they had just about given up hope of ever getting a baby. We all knew, of course, that it was impossible for Mickey to be placed in their home. First of all, he was born locally, and according to agency regulations he had to be placed in another city. Secondly, our caseworker knew that we were friends and had already told us that no baby from our home would be placed with them. But the word 'impossible' doesn't seem to be in God's vocabulary. He obviously had different ideas. Through an incredible set of circumstances, within days Mickey was their son."

"Our caseworker is also a Christian," Bruce said. "When we met at the agency to deliver Mickey to his new parents, all five of us took time to sit together in her office and pray for this new family. Now that is my definition of a truly chosen family."

Children who live in foster homes for long periods of time almost always suffer emotionally from feelings of rejection and impermanence, and many adoptive parents worry about the long-term effects. Ned Simon does not share their worry.

"Beth and I know that Jonathan and Tamara may have memories of their early lives," he says. "And there is a good chance that they will run into some of their birth relatives here in town. In fact it's already happened. We have even discussed how we would feel if, as adults, they should decide to return to their birth families. I don't think there's much chance of that happening, but I suppose it could. The way I see it, no one has any guarantees about the future. It's in the hands of the Lord. But whatever happens, we know that for now our kids are exactly where God wants them—right here in our home. Our lives have certainly been a lot happier and more fulfilled because of Jonathan and Tamara."

There are many children without families of their own. Some, especially the babies, will be adopted right away. Others will wait and wait, but eventually the right family will claim them. But what about the rest? They will spend their entire childhood in a system of foster care. They will be shifted from family to family, from home to home. They will never know the deep love, the security, the warmth, and the permanence that real parents and a real family can offer. What will become of them?

OPEN FORUM

GREG SWANSON: *We thought we wanted children but we had so little prior experience with them that we didn't feel right about making a positive commitment. Our social worker suggested foster care as a training ground.*

VICTORIA MEYERS: *Is it really the same?*

LORRAINE SWANSON: *Not exactly, but it gives you an idea of all that is involved in the daily care of a child.*

BEN MEYERS: *I thought that most foster children weren't free to be adopted.*

LORRAINE SWANSON: *They aren't. The social worker warned us not to accept a foster child with the idea of adopting him or her. Only occasionally does that work out. It was just a way for us to see if we really wanted to be parents and, if so, what kind of child we would be willing to take.*

GREG SWANSON: *Our first two children were older. We got along all right with both of them, but we would never have wanted to adopt either one. The third had a medical problem which we found we could easily live with.*

LORRAINE SWANSON: *Experience in foster care is especially important for someone who is considering adopting a child with a handicap.*

QUESTIONS FOR DISCUSSION:

1. What characteristics do you think are important in a foster parent?
2. In what ways can foster care help you make your decision concerning adoption?

9. *My Brother's Keeper*

"It was a rainy Sunday in November when my mother called to tell us that Danny had been freed for adoption," said Rita Zimmerman, a woman of forty. "Danny was the three-year-old son of my sister-in-law's cousin Sharon.

"In the small town where I was raised, Sharon was considered the black sheep in a family of—shall I say—questionable reputation. She and her husband, both on drugs, were married at fifteen. Danny was born a month later. That poor boy spent his first three years in an awful home situation. On one particular day he was in the hospital and his father was in jail on charges of child abuse. But in Sharon's eyes all the problems were 'that bratty little kid's fault,' and she wanted Danny out of her life for good.

"Since my husband Norm and I had been married for almost ten years and we still had no children, my mother suggested that day that we might consider adopting Danny. We had exactly one week to make up our minds. Norm and I left that night to drive the nine hundred miles to my mother's house.

"When we got to the hospital and met Danny, it was love at first sight. Despite his black eye and the cast on his arm, he was a feisty little guy just bursting with energy. Norm spent hours playing and laughing with him. My husband was the very picture of a proud papa. We didn't need a week to decide. We wanted Danny to be our son.

"I was every bit as thrilled at becoming a mother as Norm was at becoming a father," Rita continued. "But the thrill ended abruptly on our way back home. That trip was pure torture. Danny wouldn't have a thing to do with me. He cried when I looked at him, and he screamed when I touched him. Norm was the one he liked. Finally in embarrassment and exasperation I told Norm to pull over to the side of the road. I drove the rest of the way home while Norm played Mommy."

"When we got home, however, Danny adjusted to us very quickly," Norm added. "The problem was his overprotectiveness. When my mother came for a weekend visit, he refused to let her step into his room. Nor would he let her touch either Rita or me. Fortunately that didn't last too long."

"Although he seems to have no recollection of those first three years, Danny has always known that he was adopted," Rita said. "It would have been foolish to try to keep it from him. He also knows who his birth parents are and why they couldn't keep him. He hasn't met them yet, but I'm sure it's just a matter of time until their paths cross.

"Danny's biological grandmother has been our biggest problem," Rita added with a sigh. "Danny stays with her for two weeks every summer, and she spends the entire time telling him how much she wishes he lived with her. According to Grandma, she begged to adopt him herself but wasn't allowed to because she was too sickly. She moans about how lonely she is and how she just lives for those two weeks each year when Danny is with her. By the time he gets back home, he's suffering terribly from depression and a deep sense of guilt.

"But Danny's grandmother's version of the story is less than accurate, to put it charitably. The truth is that several times during those first three years Sharon begged her mother to take Danny. But Grandma wasn't interested. She suggested that her grandson be put into a foster home; she wasn't about to let that little boy cramp her style.

"Last summer, when Danny was seven, he came from his yearly visit talking endlessly about how much his grandmother loves him and how badly she wanted to keep him. The more he talked, the more irritated I became. Later that day, when I scolded him about something, he yelled, 'Grandma never treats me like you do! I should've stayed with her!' Without thinking I snapped back, 'If you think you would be so much happier with your grandmother, why don't you go back?' I immediately regretted saying that, but I get so angry with his grandmother that I can't think straight. Maybe I should just tell Danny the truth about her."

"I can certainly understand Rita's frustration," said Norm Zimmerman, "but I don't think she should talk to Danny about his grandmother. For one thing, he probably wouldn't believe a thing Rita said. I think we should approach the problem by going directly to his grandmother. If she won't cooperate, we should simply put an end to the visits. I don't think Danny really cares that much about going anyway. There's very little for him to do there, and he always comes home so upset. At any rate, he's bound to learn the truth about her eventually. It's common knowledge among the relatives."

Special problems such as the Zimmermans were experiencing arise when the adopted child is a family member. John and Ruth Cornelius, who adopted their six-year-old grandson Ricky eight years ago, have the added problem of regular contact between Ricky and his birth mother, their daughter.

"Our daughter was a rebellious girl," Ruth said. "She was only fifteen when Ricky was born. Soon afterward, against our advice, she married her child's father and they both dropped out of school. They couldn't find jobs, so they lived on welfare, which suited them just fine. They partied all night and slept all day. Ricky was terribly neglected. John and I did all we could, but it was awfully hard. Our daughter was always accusing us of trying to run her life. After four years her husband moved out, and he hasn't been seen or heard from since.

"Ricky had been with us off and on since he was a baby. By the time he was five he was here more than he was with his mother. When the time came for him to start school, I talked my daughter into letting him live with us permanently. We adopted him the following year.

"Our daughter is around now and then," Ruth continued. "She tells Ricky that she's his real mother. That just seems to add to his feelings of abandonment and rejection. She tells him that she loves him, then she disappears for months at a time. She tells him that he's always in her thoughts, but she has yet to remember him on his birthday or at Christmas. She says she cares about him, but she's never once taken care of him when he was sick. She tells him that she's a Christian and that she wants him to be a Christian, too, but she lives like the devil."

Ruth paused to wipe away a tear. "She's my daughter, and I will always love her, but I would rather never see her again than to have her around hurting Ricky. So why can't I bring myself to throw her out?"

"At first I wasn't too happy about having Ricky with us on

a permanent basis," said John Cornelius. "Ruth and I worked hard at raising our own children. Ricky was our daughter's problem. I felt too old and too tired to start over again with another little one. But now I can't imagine life without that boy. He has made me young again. And I'm good for Ricky too. I'm older and much wiser now. How can I help but be a better parent?"

SOMETIMES IT DOESN'T WORK OUT

Despite the difficulties, the Zimmermans and the Corneliuses are optimistic about their chances of successfully integrating Danny and Ricky into their families. But Tim and Ingrid Wolff are not so sure.

"Brian and Kara are my sister's children," Ingrid explained. "I had never met them because they lived in another state. But even my sister admitted that they had real emotional problems. When her off-again, on-again marriage finally ended, my sister asked me to take her children. The judge at their custody hearing ruled that neither she nor her husband was a fit parent and that the children would have to be put into foster homes unless Tim and I agreed to take them. Under the circumstances, how could we refuse?

"From the very beginning it was a difficult situation. Brian was fourteen and Kara was eleven, exactly the ages of our own children. Our two considered their cousins a disruptive intrusion into our happy home. Having never experienced normal family life, Brian and Kara had no idea how to react to us or how to start trying to fit in. Because of their neglected upbringing, they had never developed healthy personalities or a sense of self-worth. But we tried. To the best of our ability, we truly did try."

"I felt sorry for Ingrid," Tim said. "She was always walking a tightrope between 'them' and 'us,' trying hard to please everyone. But that was an impossible undertaking. No matter how much she did for Brian and Kara, they demanded more. Because she wanted them to feel as if they belonged, she gave in to them more than she should have. Then our own children began to act up. They demanded to know why their mother preferred their cousins over them. It was a no-win situation."

"When Brian and Kara had been with us for fifteen stormy months," Ingrid continued, "my sister called to say that she and her ex-husband both felt that Tim and I were giving their children a better life than either of them could ever provide. In tears, she begged us to adopt them. I was so shocked that I couldn't think straight. I put her off by saying I'd have to talk it over with Tim and our children. Well, we did talk it over. The unanimous consensus was that, considering the shakiness of our temporary arrangement, it would be foolish to go ahead with a permanent commitment.

"That was a year ago. Brian and Kara are still with us. Although there are still a lot of unresolved problems, they have settled in a bit more comfortably and we feel more as if they are a part of our family. Gradually we have come to understand that no matter how rough things are, they can get better. Nothing that happens is truly fatal. There are solutions, and we can find them."

STEPFAMILY ADOPTIONS

According to recent statistics, one of every five children will be affected by a divorce in his family. Because 85 percent of divorcés remarry within five years, the number of stepparents in our society is increasing rapidly. This condition has brought a whole new set of adoptive circumstances. Many Christian parents and stepparents are especially anxious to gain permanent custody of their children so that they can be raised in a Christian home.

"I was still unmarried at the age of thirty-six," said Diane Cruz. "I had accepted the fact that God had called me to a single life. Then I met Luis. He had just moved to town with his two children, and he was visiting our singles group at church. I was attracted to him immediately. He seemed gentle and warm. And I could see that his relationship with the Lord was an important part of his life. But I never dreamed that he would notice me."

"How could I help but notice her?" Luis Cruz laughed.

"Diane was the only person in that class who wasn't trying to impress everyone else with her great wisdom and insights. I knew right away that I wanted to get to know her better."

"We got to know each other better, all right," Diane laughed. "After dating for a year we had a lovely Christmas wedding. Luis's children, six-year-old Denise and nine-year-old Todd, were in our wedding party.

"Todd and Denise's mother had made no effort to see them for over three years. I wanted to adopt the children right away because I was concerned about their welfare should anything happen to Luis. The problem was to find their mother and get her approval. When we were finally able to locate her, she offered no resistance.

"The children were outspoken about their desire to be with us, and we felt like a family from the very beginning. Many people have asked me how Todd and Denise were able to make such a quick and painless adjustment. I've given it a lot of thought and have decided that there were three important factors. First, instead of suddenly springing the idea of our marriage on the children, Luis and I included them in our relationship from the very beginning. Second, at the ages of six and nine the children were still young enough to be fairly adaptable. Third and most important, the foundation and controlling base of our family is God's providential love and care for all of us.

"When we had been married for three years," Diane continued, "God blessed us with a new baby. Though I loved Todd and Denise dearly, I worried throughout my pregnancy that I would love this new baby more. I'm pleased to say that my fears were groundless. The baby is no more my real child than the other two are. But my family can't quite understand this. The first Mother's Day after the baby was born I got a card from my sister. On it she had written, 'For your first Mother's Day as a real mother.' After looking at it for a minute, Todd tossed the card aside and snorted, 'Aunt Janine doesn't know what a real mother is!'"

As Diane herself acknowledged, the Cruz family had a lot going for it. Most blended families are not so fortunate.

When a child leaves his old family life behind and begins a new one, he cannot help but bring along his old habits, behavior, and ways of doing things. The adults involved will do the same. The problem is that one person's way of doing things won't be the same as someone else's. Everyone is bringing his own memories, his own confusion, his own fears and scars into this new family. It will take time for them to blend together into one cohesive group.

A child who is shifted from one parent to another, or from one relationship to another, has to face some monumental questions and fears. Whether by death or divorce, the child has experienced a breakup in his family. There is risk in letting himself become attached to this new person: will he or she also leave? Moreover, the new stepparent has different expectations. Can the child ever hope to please everyone? To whom should he be loyal anyway—to his birth parent or his stepparent?

When problems appear in a stepchild—whether distrust, indifference, withdrawal, hostility, or rebellion—it's important to remember that the child is in a very difficult situation not of his own making. It is hardly surprising that, as an innocent and helpless victim, he would protest in any way he can.

And what about the stepparent? Even though he may really want to see a feeling of love and belonging develop between himself and the stepchild, he may discover that it's not all that easy to accomplish. Though the stepparent wants the child to adapt, too often he's not willing to do the same. Compromise is essential, and it's a two-way street. It is neither realistic nor fair to expect a child to conform completely to the stepparent's expectations.

What can a stepparent do to help the family achieve a smooth, happy adjustment? There are no sure answers to this question, but there are some factors that will make it easier for everyone.

- Be sure that the child is prepared for the marriage and the adjustments that will be necessary. Assure him that you will all work together to find solutions for any problems that arise;
- It is important that you settle some matters with your spouse before the wedding so that you can present a united and consistent front. It is vital that you agree on

such things as priorities, expectations, and approaches to discipline. Be willing to compromise; it's essential;

- Don't attempt to make any major changes right away. You must first allow time for everyone to get used to the new arrangement;

- Resist the temptation to denigrate the missing parent. Don't try to compete with him or her. Instead, point out the importance of appreciating the uniqueness that can be found in every person;

- Above all, be patient with your stepchild. Cinderella, Hansel and Gretel, Sleeping Beauty, and a host of other personages have taught him that it's dangerous to trust a stepparent. It's up to you to prove them wrong.

LOVE MUST BE EARNED

Love doesn't just happen. It cannot be legislated or demanded. It has to be earned through time and lots of hard work.

When Ed and Donna Jackson were married, it was the second time for both. Donna had three daughters and Ed had three sons. Neither Ed nor Donna was a Christian.

"I was married at sixteen and divorced at twenty-one," Donna related. "Four years later I married Ed. My daughters— Sarah, Ashley, and Christy—were eight, six, and four. Ed's sons were older: Paul was twelve, Jason was nine, and Nicholas was seven. The boys lived with their mother thirty miles away."

"Donna and I had been married for two years when a friend invited us to a weekend couples' conference at a Christian campground," Ed Jackson said. "We had no idea what to expect, but since it was free we agreed to go. That weekend we both came to know Jesus Christ as our Savior. We immediately got involved in a great church and a group Bible study.

"As I grew in the Lord, I began to feel worse and worse about my boys growing up devoid of any Christian influence. What chance would they ever have to know the Lord? I was suddenly consumed with a great desire to have my boys with me. But that seemed impossible. I'd never be able to talk my ex-wife into giving them up. Together Donna and I sought the Lord's wisdom and guidance.

"It was Donna who suggested that we try to 'conquer with kindness.' You should have seen us! We went out of our way to be considerate and cooperative toward my former wife. Whenever she wanted to drop the boys off for a day or a weekend—which was often—we were ready to take them, even though it usually meant upsetting our own plans. After a while they were here more than they were with her. One day my ex-wife called and said, 'I hate to admit it, Ed, but you're a better father than I am a mother. I really think you love those boys more than I do. Maybe they'd be better off with you.' That's all there was to it! How's that for an answer to prayer?"

"After the boys came to live with us, people started calling us 'The Brady Bunch,' " Donna said. "But believe me, our problems were neither as amusing nor as easily solved as those television problems were. And somehow we never seemed to have the witty wisdom at our fingertips that those parents always had.

"When we became a 'blended family,' Paul was fourteen, Jason was eleven, Sarah was ten, Nicholas was nine, Ashley was eight, and Christy was six. We worked hard at establishing a pattern of candor, cooperation, and communication among all eight of us. It was hard to keep from bursting into tears when someone glibly offered criticism in an especially sensitive area. So, because Ed and I recognized the serious adjustments ahead for all of us, we tried to impress the kids with the need to temper their candor with love and consideration for one another's feelings. Together we worked out rules for the household and decided what discipline would be applied if those rules were broken."

"Paul, Jason, and Nicholas came to us with no idea of what to expect," Ed said. "They were confused and afraid, but they also had some pretty wild, unrealistic expectations. And they had memories—some pleasant, but many quite painful. Nicholas felt at home right away. He loved Donna and he loved me. Jason's adjustment was not quite so easy, but he did adjust. Paul, however, became obnoxious. He began testing us the day he arrived and never stopped. He made life especially miserable for Donna."

The pain showed on Donna's face as she said, "There was a time when I honestly believed that with enough love I could overcome any obstacle. I don't believe that anymore. If a child doesn't want to become a part of a family, no one can force him to do it. The child must adopt his parents every bit as much as his parents must adopt him."

"I'm certain that a lot of Paul's problems were caused by the conflicting loyalties he felt," Ed said thoughtfully. "I can understand that. He had lived with his mother for most of his life.

"Finally, in desperation Donna and I took Paul to a counselor. Unfortunately we didn't give much thought to the man we chose. He was a counselor whose main philosophy was that a person's primary concern should be his own happiness and comfort. He told Paul that he should have free run of the house without any restrictions from us. He even went so far as to scold Donna and me for undermining Paul's creative ambitions by disciplining him. Can you believe it? Of course, we never went back to that counselor again. But the damage was already done. What little control I had over Paul was gone.

"When he was sixteen, Paul ran away and went back to live with his mother. She made the most of the situation. Paul quit school and found a full-time job. His mother took his paychecks to help pay off her stack of overdue bills. At night, while she went out with her boyfriends, Paul served as a free baby-sitter for her three-year-old.

"It wasn't long before Paul got fed up with that arrangement. He was back in our home in two months. But his heart wasn't with us. Whenever anything happened that didn't suit him, he was off again. Finally I had to decide whether it was right to risk sacrificing my marriage and the emotional well-being of the other five children in a seemingly futile effort to help Paul. What could I do but commit him to the Lord and then let him go? Last year I had to make the most difficult decision of my life: I had my son put into a foster home."

"Wherever he goes and whatever he does," Donna said thoughtfully, "Paul is surrounded by our love and our prayers. I'm sure that in time he'll come around. When he does, we will be waiting for him with open arms."

After a pause Donna added, "When we talk to the kids about the importance of living for the Lord while they are young, they sometimes point to our own lives and say, 'When you were our age you did all the things you tell us not to do, but everything worked out all right for you, didn't it?' I truly believe that God allowed our heartbreaking situation with Paul so that the other children will see that Ed and I didn't get off scot-free. Where there is sin, its consequences are sure to follow."

"That's not to say that Paul had no choice in his actions," Ed quickly added. "Of course he did. But the fact remains that I wasn't there during his formative years. The Bible speaks of the sins of fathers being visited upon their children. This is hard for us to accept even though we see it again and again."

Long ago Cain asked the question, "Am I my brother's keeper?" For the Jacksons, the answer is yes. The Cruzes and the Wolffs agree. So do the Corneliuses and the Zimmermans. But taking in a relative and making him your own is not always an easy thing to do. It takes patience, determination, understanding love, and a great deal of dependence upon the Lord.

"All children need loving guidance," said Donna Jackson. "That's the whole idea of parenting: love, understanding, and honesty. If your family has these, it doesn't matter whether the child is yours, mine, or ours.

"Our family has a special verse that we claim as our own. It's Colossians 2:6: 'And now just as you trusted Christ to save you, trust Him too for each day's problems.' What more can we ask?"

OPEN FORUM

JACK KELLEY: *Cheryl and I have both been married before, and we both brought children into our marriage. We have had some real heartrending experiences when our kids have come home from a visit with their other parents completely elated by the good time they had. But when it really comes down to it, they know that we're their parents. Their hearts are with us. Without realizing it, we have brought on much of our own pain. We've put ourselves through unnecessary anguish.*

DR. MCDILL: *We all do that at times, don't we? But the very fact that your children came home and talked freely to you is a credit to your good parenting.*

JACK KELLEY: *We encouraged them to talk and to share their experiences with us. We felt that the more open we were in allowing them to express themselves, the better it would be for all of us. The less we tried to influence their feelings, the better it worked out and the more honest they were with us.*

DR. MCDILL: *How right you are! We all so badly need that openness.*

CHERYL KELLEY: *Our oldest kids are sixteen and eighteen, and they know all about their father. He's not as bad as some, I suppose, but he surely is no trophy. We do not approve of his lifestyle, and when the boys were in their early teens we wouldn't let them see him at all. That really caused problems and rebellion. Since they resented our trying to tell them what their father was like, we decided that they needed to see it for themselves. We called him and, through clenched teeth, told him that we would like him to spend some time with his sons.*

DR. MCDILL: *If you had it to do again, would you do anything differently?*

JACK KELLEY: *I think we would allow the relationship with their father to develop more naturally. He wasn't really that interested in them anyway, so he wouldn't have taken the trouble to see them more than once or twice a year. Maybe then it wouldn't have become such an obsession with them.*

CHERYL KELLEY: *Two years ago we had drug problems with one of the boys. But as soon as we let him get to know his father, the problems virtually disappeared.*

JACK KELLEY: *Not knowing his father really bothered that boy. He used to say, "The man could die or lose a leg, and I wouldn't even know about it!"*

CHERYL KELLEY: *The eighteen-year-old can go out with his father and have a nice time, but he can also see that in many ways he is actually more mature than his father is. Even the sixteen-year-old is beginning to see the reality. Lately he's been saying, "Don't worry, Mom. I don't want to be like him." We don't like the idea of this man influencing our boys, but we grit our teeth and pray that whatever limited influence he does have won't wipe out the years of influence we have had.*

103

JACK KELLEY: *Kids actually are quite resilient and perceptive. We're teaching our children God's Word and His wisdom. Now we must trust God to bring them safely to adulthood.*

QUESTIONS FOR DISCUSSION

1. What special problems does a family who adopts a relative have?
2. Do you think Ed and Donna Jackson could have done anything to help Paul adjust to their new blended family?
3. How could the Jacksons have gone about making a better choice in a counselor? (Also see chapter 12.)

10. *A Parent Alone*

"I like children," said Jackie Schulman, a twenty-five-year-old, self-employed piano tuner. "I'm not married—maybe I never will be—but I think I'd make a super mother.

"In an evening music class I became acquainted with a single woman who adopted an eight-year-old orphan from Brazil. The two of them share a house with another single woman who also has an adopted child. Talking to this lady and seeing how well things have worked out for her has made me think seriously about adopting a little girl of my own.

"When I called the adoption agency to ask about the proper procedure for such an adoption, I could hardly get anyone to talk to me. I was quite bluntly informed that if I ever were to get approved—which was doubtful in itself—I would be placed at the bottom of their list of prospective parents because I'm single.

"I had it all worked out. My best friend and I share a rented house, and there is plenty of room for a child. Though I'm certainly not rich, my income would easily be enough to support myself and a little girl. My working hours are flexible and could be adjusted around the child's school hours. But no one seemed interested in hearing my qualifications. It was never said in so many words, but the answer that came across to me was 'Forget it. We aren't in the market for single parents.'"

A single person will undoubtedly have a more difficult time obtaining a child than a couple will.*

Jackie Schulman had very little going for her as a potential adoptive parent. First, she was too young. Women in their late thirties and forties are preferred because it is felt that by then a

*Most singles who want to adopt children are women. Agencies that place children with single people indicate that women outnumber men twenty-five to one as adoptive parents.

person is more likely to be comfortable with his or her singleness and ready to settle down with a child to enjoy the daily routines of domestic life. Second, Jackie's financial base was not adequately stable. With almost no savings, her income depended entirely on her ability to find work consistently. Third, although she had thought about adjusting her hours to coincide with the child's time in school, she had not taken into consideration summer vacations, school holidays, and times when the child would need to stay home because of illness. Fourth, Jackie is a renter. Agencies definitely prefer and sometimes insist that their adoptive parents be homeowners. Fifthly, because all of Jackie's close friends are unmarried women, she has no way of surrounding a child with good two-parent family models or with consistent male companionship. Even her own family has little to offer in this respect.

But even if Jackie were an older, financially secure homeowner who was surrounded by happy two-parent families, her struggle to have a child placed in her home would be far from easy. The goal of almost all adoption agencies is to place every child in a stable, two-parent home. They know that parenting a child alone is difficult. Nevertheless, the trend is toward more single-parent adoptions, at least with hard-to-place children or children from other countries.

Asked whether her agency accepted applications from single persons, a social worker in charge of placement said, "We certainly do. In fact we have some children available who we feel might more easily adjust to a single-parent home." Then she explained that despite the increase in single-parent adoptions in recent years, these placements are still relatively few in number.

Many criteria are important for a single person who wants to adopt. She must have experience with children and fully understand all that is involved in child care. She must realize that parenting is a twenty-four-hour-a-day, seven-day-a-week job. She must be healthy, both physically and emotionally. She must be realistic and mature. She must have financial security, for she will be the child's sole provider. This includes making an adequate arrangement for day care while she is at work, especially for those times when the child is ill.

The first question an adoptive parent must ask herself is

"What can I do for this child?" not "What can this child do for me?" Many times a prospective single parent is trying to meet her own need for companionship. While this is an understandable need, it is not an adequate reason to seek to adopt. The only acceptable motivation is an earnest desire to love and care for a child.

DISCOURAGING CIRCUMSTANCES

Discouraged by her circumstances, Jackie Schulman abandoned the idea of adoption. Sheila Carswell, however, had good reason to persist. A thirty-seven-year-old elementary schoolteacher who was obviously comfortable in her role as a single adult, Sheila came much closer to fitting the picture of an ideal single parent.

"When I approached a private adoption agency about the possibility of adopting a child, I realized that such a placement would be neither quick nor easy," Sheila said. "But I was convinced that I would be a good mother, so I was determined to try. I appreciated the realistic honesty of the social worker with whom I spoke. She warned me at the outset that among adoption applicants, the prospective single parent is at the bottom of the heap. Agencies prefer good two-parent families.

"I didn't ask for an infant or a toddler, because I know that such children are easily placed with couples. And since I'm a schoolteacher, a school-aged child would fit more easily into my life. Not only our hours but also our vacations would be the same. If the child should have to miss school because of illness, my sick leave would allow me the time off to care for her.

"The social worker who interviewed me asked questions about every imaginable area of my life. Some of the questions were really incredible! Why hadn't I ever married? Would I marry if someone were to ask me? How stable did I consider myself? What was my real reason for wanting a child? What needs could I meet in a child better than someone else could? How would I manage to raise a child by myself? What kind of a child would I accept? These are just a few of the dozens of questions that were fired at me.

"When the social worker finally told me that in her estimation I was well qualified and emotionally prepared to become a single parent, I heaved a sigh of relief. Then she told me about a couple of little girls who were available but because of their ages, nationalities, or physical problems would have little chance of ever being placed for adoption. 'It just may be,' she said, 'that one of those girls is the right one for you.'

"From the very beginning, my parents and two younger sisters were against my plans to adopt," Sheila explained. "They were afraid that everyone who met me and my child would automatically assume that I had been divorced or, even worse, that my child was illegitimate. Again and again they chided me for refusing to accept being a single, childless schoolteacher as my lot in life.

"The counselors at the agency felt that my family would have to play a major part in the life of any child I might adopt, so a social worker was sent to talk with my parents and my sisters and brothers-in-law. She sensed immediately the bitterness and hostility they felt.

"A few weeks later I was notified that my application for adoption had been turned down. According to the social worker, I had many excellent qualities and would probably have made a very good mother. My rejection, she said, was due entirely to the fact that my child and I would have received no emotional support from my family. In fact, in her opinion, they would actually have caused extra problems in an already difficult situation. I argued, I pleaded, and I explained, but the decision was final. There is little flexibility of regulations when it comes to single-parent adoptions!"

DETERMINATION THAT PAID OFF

Most single men and women who consider adoption either become discouraged at the outset and never pursue it, as in Jackie Schulman's case, or else, like Sheila Carswell, they are turned down because they fail to meet the agency's strict criteria. Only a few single people make it to the point of having a child actually placed with them. When it does happen, it is a real testimony to the resilience and determination of the adoptive parent. Or, as Juanita Hart says, it is a real testimony to the providential hand of God.

"I have two adopted children," said Juanita, a reporter for a major metropolitan newspaper. "Robin, who was four when I got her, is now fourteen; Andy, adopted as an infant, is almost seven. God was preparing the way for me to get my children long before I had any thought of adopting or any way of doing so.

"After graduating from college, I left my North Dakota farm home and came to Los Angeles to seek my fortune in the big city. I started attending a small church, where I was befriended by a widow by the name of Betty Morgan. She was about my mother's age.

"My big plans and dreams were soon shattered when I found that I couldn't even get an interview, much less a job, with the local newspaper. Broke and discouraged, I was ready to forget my dreams, swallow my pride, and go back home—a failure at the age of twenty-three. But Betty wouldn't hear of it. She encouraged me, listened to me, sympathized with me, advised me, and plied me with free home-cooked meals.

"When I had been in Los Angeles less than a year, I contracted hepatitis. Since I was much too ill to care for myself, Betty took me in to live with her. By the time I was finally well again, I had no apartment, no job, and no money. So I stayed on with Betty.

"The next year, after I succeeded in landing a job as a rookie reporter, the rent on our apartment was raised so drastically that we could no longer afford to stay there. Betty had some money in the bank, and at her suggestion we used it as a down payment on a little house. Shortly afterward a friend of Betty's asked us to keep three thousand dollars of her money in our bank account. She wanted to protect the money from her alcoholic husband. The result was a padded account that made us look much wealthier than we were.

"By this time I was twenty-six years old and was doing well in my job at the newspaper. Betty, however, was bored with staying home alone all day. She was also feeling guilty about not being able to contribute to the house payments. So she suggested that we take in a foster child.

"It sounded like a great idea to me. I've always loved

children. Our home was approved, and within two months four-year-old Robin was brought to us.

"Robin was a victim of child abuse. This was the fourth time that she had been removed from her mother. Each time previously Robin had been returned to her, but this time was the worst ever. The bruised and bleeding little girl had watched in terror as her mother was handcuffed and dragged, kicking and screaming, into a police car. Robin spent three hours being stitched up and bandaged in a hospital emergency room. She arrived at our house confused, frightened, and hurting. She cried all night.

"By morning Robin had settled down. She told me, 'The policeman said he would find me a really nice mommy. You must be her.' From then on I was 'Mommy' and Betty was 'Grandmommy.'

"Robin loved Betty and me, and we adored her," Juanita continued. "We took her everywhere we went even though she was never really comfortable outside the house. As soon as we came home, she would run inside and cry, 'Mommy, Mommy, lock the door!'

"Although all her family lived within twenty miles of our house, two whole months went by before any relative made an effort to contact her. They just didn't seem to be interested. When her mother and grandmother finally did come—unannounced—Robin would not go near them. She was terrified that they had come to take her away. They were granted visitation rights, but Robin steadfastly refused to see them. Even when I picked her up and carried her into the room where they were, she totally ignored them, acting as if they weren't there. She wouldn't even open the gifts they brought her. Naturally they wouldn't accept any responsibility for her feelings toward them. Instead they blamed me, claiming that I was deliberately turning her against them.

"Practically every day Robin would ask me, 'Do you promise you'll be my mommy forever?' I can't tell you how badly I wanted to make her that promise, but how could I? Even though both Betty and I wanted to adopt Robin, her mother wouldn't release her—especially not to me. Moreover, her mother called me one night in a drunken rage and screamed, 'You'd better never take my daughter away from me! If you do,

I'll fix you for good!' I don't know where that woman is now—
she had been in and out of prison—but I can tell you that we
have really had to commit ourselves to the Lord's care and
safekeeping.

"Our case worker was well aware of my desire to adopt
Robin," said Juanita. "She warned me that if I didn't fight hard
for her, Robin was sure to be returned once again to her family.
The caseworker helped me by accumulating evidence that
Robin's family was unfit to raise her. It took several years, but
finally, by court order, Robin was declared free for adoption.

"Now this is the exciting part! Listen to how the Lord's
providential preparations all came together so that we could
keep Robin. Because Betty was able to be home twenty-four
hours a day, and because Betty and I had bought the house, and
because I had a ready-made 'extended family' in my group of
friends at church, and because we still had the other woman's
money in our bank account, I was approved as an adoptive
single parent. It took more than four years, but at the age of
nine Robin was legally declared my daughter.

"From the time Robin first arrived, everything in our house
revolved around her," Juanita continued. "When she was seven
years old, I began to feel that she would really benefit by having
another child around. Our foster home was licensed for three
children, so Betty and I decided to ask for another child. I
didn't want anyone who would compete with Robin, however.
She was still too fragile emotionally for that. Rather, I wanted
someone she could love and help care for, someone who could
teach her the joys of giving. So we decided to ask for a baby boy.

"When I told our social worker what we had in mind, she
actually laughed out loud and said, 'You're crazy! The agency
will *never* place a baby boy with you.' But the Lord had put it in
my heart that this was what He had for us, so every morning
and every evening Betty and Robin and I prayed together that
God would give us our baby boy. We had to wait and pray for
six months, but finally it happened. Our social worker called
one morning and said, 'You win! Your baby boy is ready for
you. Shall I bring him over?' What a silly question! All three of
us were waiting on the front porch when she arrived.

"But the baby who was placed in my arms was not the
baby I had pictured for all those months. Four-week-old

Malcolm Alfonse was not an attractive infant. His skinny little body was filthy and full of sores. His head was covered with an awful case of ringworm. When he arrived, he was crying at the top of his lungs, an activity he continued almost nonstop for two whole weeks. For a long time Robin stood and stared in silence at this pitiful little creature. After all our praying, I felt that she was terribly disappointed. Finally she spoke. 'Malcolm Alfonse?' she asked. 'He looks more like an Andy to me.' And from then on, he was Andy.

"It's hard to believe, but at the tender age of four weeks Andy was already a veteran of two foster homes and one adoptive home. In his short life he had been abused, neglected, and rejected. Finally, because no one else seemed to want him, he was offered to us.

"But that little fellow was the best thing that ever happened to Robin. Perhaps because he had been so mistreated and unwanted, she could really identify with him. But they also looked alike. I'm a blue-eyed blond and Betty is very gray, but both Robin and Andy have raven-black hair and dark brown eyes. One night I tiptoed into Robin's room to kiss her goodnight. There she was with little Andy all snuggled in bed with her. Looking up at me, she said, 'Andy and I belong together, don't we, Mom?' We were just finding out what God had known all along.

"When Andy had been with us for a year, I told his caseworker that I would like to adopt him. She was irate. 'There is no way I would allow you to adopt that little boy,' she fumed. 'There isn't even a man in your house. What makes you think that you can take in foster children and then automatically adopt them? I'm going to remove him from your home immediately!'

"I was shocked by her reaction, and I was terrified that she might actually make good on her threat," Juanita continued. "But God had put Andy in our home, and no one could take him away without God's permission. Again Betty and Robin and I, along with our Christian friends, banded together in prayer. If God wanted Andy with us, He would have to intervene. If He didn't want us to keep Andy, He would have to give us the strength to accept His will and to give our baby up.

"Then, completely unsolicited, Robin's caseworker stepped

in on our behalf. Praising Robin's extraordinary adjustment, she recommended that I be allowed to adopt Andy. The agency had already approved me as an adoptive parent for Robin, so what could they say? So Andy joined our family. God had done it again!"

THE STRUGGLE GOES ON

In our society, where one out of every three marriages ends in divorce, millions of children are being raised in single-parent families. The children who are adopted by a single parent are sometimes more fortunate than those others, for they at least are spared the trauma of going through a divorce. Then too, their single parents have been hand-picked for their ability to cope with single parenthood.

But the fact remains that very few single people have the tenacity and the determination to fight for the right to adoptive parenthood. For a single person, the decision to adopt is complicated by the fact that the children who are placed in such homes are generally those who have little chance of being placed elsewhere. These children often have emotional scars that take a long, long time to heal. Isn't it ironic that single parents, who confront the difficult task of raising a child alone, are usually given the children who need the most help?

Today the major qualification for prospective adoptive parents, single or married, is that they have the potential for helping children to develop into sound, mature adults. The difference is that the single person is far less likely to get the chance to parent a child.

QUESTIONS FOR DISCUSSION

1. Under what circumstances might a single parent be the family of choice for an adoptive child?
2. Do you think that Sheila Carswell should have continued her quest for a child through another agency or through an independent adoption? How might she have gone about it?

11.
Growing Together

Every family has its own story, unique and special. It has its own dreams and hopes, its own triumphs and shared joys. It also has problems, disappointments, and struggles. And every family changes. As each member grows and develops, so does the family as a whole. This is the way families are, and those that include adopted children are no different.

In this chapter we look at some of the issues that are sure to arise as your family lives and grows together. It is vital that the lines of communication between you and your child be kept open so that there can always be a means for honest, loving, tolerant sharing. Many problems generally associated with adoption can be avoided or minimized by sharing your feelings, by listening when your child wants to talk, and by answering his questions as honestly as you can.

If you maintain an open family relationship, the time will come when your child will ask questions about adoption. Your approach to these questions should be no different than to his questions about human relationships, sex, faith, and other issues of growing and learning. Present the answers comfortably and truthfully. Don't worry about the actual words; they are not nearly so important as the feelings and attitudes you communicate. Even without eloquent explanations you can communicate your love to your child. You can let him know that he belongs with you and that you are glad he does.

One of the first concerns many adoptive parents face is whether or not to tell their child that she is adopted. Today almost all adoption authorities agree that the child should be told. If you don't tell her, sooner or later she will probably find it out from someone else. Such a disclosure is tragic and unfair and could give your child the impression that you are ashamed of the adoption. It will also undermine your credibility. After all, if you weren't honest with your child about something as important as his adoption, how can she trust you to be honest about anything else?

The easiest and most successful way of handling the matter is to deal with it as an accepted fact of family life. It is important that your child be allowed to grow up with this knowledge. From the beginning her adoption should be an open, accepted, and understood fact. Talk about it from time to time in a casual, matter-of-fact way that is natural and comfortable for you.

You need not go into detail at first. Your child will not understand and will not be interested. It is enough for her to hear the word "adoption" and to associate it with warmth, comfort, security, and love. She will let you know when she is ready for more information by asking more questions. Follow her lead.

Be careful, however, not to carry your talk of adoption too far. Overemphasizing it can be just as bad as ignoring it. If you are always talking about your child's adoption, you will be emphasizing that he is different. This is certain to make him uncomfortable. The key is to strike a balance. Don't remind him too much, but mention it often enough to be sure that the idea is accepted and natural.

OPEN FORUM

KAREN ALVARADO: *The older of our two adopted children is three. I feel that I probably should be telling her about her adoption, but I just don't know when or how to do it.*

TERRY COHEN: *Don and I started using the word "adoption" when our daughter was just a baby. Then, when we thought she was old enough to understand, we explained what adoption meant. I think she was about three years old at the time.*

DON COHEN: *If you wait too long, your child may hear it from someone else first.*

KAREN ALVARADO: *Sometimes I actually forget that she is adopted.*

KEN RANDLE: *It sounds to me as if you may be uncomfortable with the word "adoption." Our approach was to be free in our use of the word. We didn't go out of our way to use it constantly, but when it came up naturally, we didn't try to avoid it.*

KAREN ALVARADO: *How would my daughter know how I feel about adoption? She's only three.*

KEN RANDLE: *You would be amazed at how much little children can learn from what they overhear. They can sense your attitudes just by the way you say something or by the way you avoid saying it.*

KATHERINE O'NEILL: *Our son enjoys explaining adoption to his little sister. He can remember going with us to get her. It was a happy time for him. He tells her, "Mommy and Daddy really wanted you. We all prayed about it, and God brought you into our family."*

GREG SWANSON: *We have some books on adoption around the house for the children to look at. Not only do they encourage questions, but they also tend to give adoption an air of acceptance.*

DR. MCDILL: *I like the approach of waiting until the child asks questions. It's important to catch that moment of readiness. Otherwise you may be giving him data that he isn't ready to handle. It's better to wait for that moment of readiness than to be burdened with the dilemma of deciding when to tell, how to tell, and so forth. When the questions do come, keep the answers simple. Be prepared for that right moment with correct answers. Otherwise your child may draw a totally incorrect conclusion from your silence or hesitation.*

THE NEED
FOR UNCONDITIONAL LOVE

"I hate you! I don't like it here! I'm going to find my real mother and move in with her!"

If your adopted child has ever shouted things like this, you know how shocking, confusing, and painful such pronouncements can be. When this happens it is important to remember that it does not mean you have failed as a parent. It is easy to react to the words your child speaks and to miss his real message. When your child accuses you of not loving him or says that he doesn't love you, he is probably really asking, "Do you love me no matter what I do?" or "Are you really my parents?" or "Do you care enough to make me obey the rules?"

An adopted child, especially one who has been unwanted in the past, has an enormous need to know that he is loved unconditionally. If he doesn't have a backlog of experience that tells him he is a valuable person, he cannot take it for granted. He needs to hear you tell him so again and again. You will be able to find many opportunities to say such things as "I love you," "You look so nice today," or "You did that job so well! Thank you for helping me."

But be careful that you don't say the words unless you really mean them. Strained or phony compliments will be recognized immediately for what they are, and they will do more harm than good. Your consistent warmth, security, and loving discipline guide your child to a secure sense of belonging and to feelings of self-worth. Day by day, through your loving care, you are giving your child the emotional strength and stability he needs to face the realities that life will inevitably bring his way.

One of these realities is a possible contact with a birth mother or other relative. Many adoptive parents possess letters written by a child's biological parents at the time of birth, left with instructions that they be given to the child at a specific age. For many these letters are a real source of worry. Several of the parents with whom I spoke had questions about such letters.

OPEN FORUM

KATHERINE O'NEILL: *When we got our first child we were given a letter from his thirteen-year-old mother with instructions that it be given to him on his thirteenth birthday. She wrote that she loved his father very much but that they couldn't raise a child because they were just children themselves. She said her parents thought it would be best for her to finish school. She added that if he ever wanted to look her up, she would be happy for him to do so. Our son is now almost thirteen, and I don't really want to give the letter to him. How much do we owe the child who gave birth to our son? Must we follow her directions?*

ROGER CRAWFORD: *You have adopted the child, so he's your responsibility. You have to do what you think is best for him. You have no obligation to his birth mother.*

GREG SWANSON: *We have two letters, one to us and one to our child. The one to our child came with expressed instructions that it be presented unopened to him on his sixteenth birthday. Since we have honored her request not to open the sealed envelope, we have no idea what is in the letter.*

ROB ALVARADO: *That's a ticking time bomb!*

DR. MCDILL: *I can see very little good coming from a letter like that.*

GREG SWANSON: *We just wonder morally what we should do. The birth parents were married, and the letter she wrote to us was really neat. But the adoption agency did declare them unfit parents.*

VICTORIA MEYERS: *Since your real obligation is to your child, not to his mother, I think that you should open the letter yourself and see what it says. Then you can decide whether you want to give it to him at all.*

DR. MCDILL: *A confused, new mother—a little girl—wrote that letter. Whatever she put in it seemed appropriate at the time, but now she may feel very differently. There could be things in there that would cause great harm and damage.*

KEN RANDLE: *I couldn't justify the dishonesty of opening my child's letter. I would give it to him unopened.*

MR. DONNELLY: *I wonder if you would still feel that way if you had met with as many birth mothers as I have. They are often very confused and mixed-up. I would be concerned about what my child would find in such a letter. I agree with Victoria; I would open it and make a judgment based on its contents. But I wouldn't be hypocritical about it. I would tell my child that I disregarded the instructions because, loving him as I do, I wanted to be sure that I was doing the right thing for him.*

DR. MCDILL: *In the end you must keep in mind that your responsibility lies with the child. You must decide what you feel would be the best for him, then do it without feeling guilty.*

WHEN TEASING HURTS

"Why are children so cruel?" asked one adoptive mother. "Why do they tease adopted children so unmercifully?"

Children can be terribly thoughtless and cruel in their treatment of other children. If the teasing draws a reaction from the child, the offenders can become downright vicious. Adopted children have no corner on getting teased, however. What they do have is a sensitive area of vulnerability. When this sensitive area is attacked, a child can be hurt deeply.

OPEN FORUM

HOWARD VAUGHN: *Both of our daughters have experienced a lot of painful teasing from other children at school and a lot of jeers on the playground. Once our older daughter was told, "No wonder your real mother gave you up. You were too ugly to keep!" My daughter is actually a very lovely girl, but that comment hurt her so badly that I'm not sure the wound will ever heal completely.*

KATHERINE O'NEILL: *Once our daughter was called a derogatory variation of "illegitimate." Fortunately she talked to me about it. It so happens that she was an illegitimate child, so I took that opportunity to tell her the circumstances of her birth. But I also assured her that this had no bearing whatsoever on who she is or on her personal worth.*

DR. MCDILL: *You did the right thing. I once had a patient who came to me for counseling because she had a terrible relationship with her mother. During treatment she angrily stated, "I hate my mother because I'm illegitimate!" I was certain this wasn't true, so I asked her where she had gotten such an idea. It seems that as a young child she had overheard some older children refer to a classmate as illegitimate, so she asked her mother if she was also. Her mother just said, "What a silly question!" Since her mother hadn't actually denied it, the girl assumed it was true. You can see the damage that can be caused by failing to fully answer and discuss a child's questions.*

KEN RANDLE: *I teach in a junior high school, and I can attest to the fact that many kids say anything that pops into their heads. They don't stop to think that their remark may hurt someone else. To them it's just a joke.*

DR. MCDILL: *You cannot protect your child from hurtful comments. But you can arm him against their harmful effects by providing him with a healthy self-concept and a great reserve of love from which he can draw.*

119

IN QUEST OF THE PAST

When your child begins to ask questions about his adoption, it may distress you to find that many of them concern his biological parents. You will undoubtedly be asked, "Why did they give me up?" In answering this question it is important that you emphasize the fact that your child's being "given up" was in no way his fault. Whatever he is or is not had no bearing on his birth parents' decision to allow his adoption. Though you may know very little—maybe nothing at all—about his birth parents and their problems, you can honestly say that there were many people who cared enough about him to see that he was placed in a family that really loves and wants him. He is where he belongs: safe and sound in your home. You can also say that for some reason beyond their control, the people to whom he was born could not take care of him. You can fill in as many details as you know and feel that your child can handle at the moment.

No one sets out to be a bad parent. We all do the best we can to cope with the demands of life. But there are people who, no matter how they try, do not have the capacity to be good parents. Some realize their limitations and voluntarily relinquish the responsibility for their children. Others can only demonstrate their inability to parent, and in these cases the courts must step in and remove the child. The important thing is that it is not because no one cared about him that the child was freed for adoption.

Virtually all adopted children want to know about their birth parents—what they looked like, how old they were, their interests and talents and abilities. Some adoptive parents have a more difficult time dealing with these questions than others do. There are some who absolutely refuse to discuss their child's past, even going so far as to deny that the child is not biologically theirs.

"My daughter doesn't ask questions about her birth parents," said one mother emphatically. "She just isn't interested. She knows she's our child and that's enough for her."

Just because your adopted child doesn't talk about his past does not mean he doesn't think about it. He does. And he needs to have some explanation and answers. If you are comfortable in talking with your child about his past, he will also be comfortable. On the other hand, if he senses that raising certain questions threatens or embarrasses you, he may try to protect both you and himself by avoiding those uncomfortable subjects. You may think that you are able to hide your feelings from your child. Be careful: children understand a whole lot more than we think they do.

A child's ability to handle information about his background changes as he matures. Eventually, as an adult, he should have all the information you have, even though his birth parents may have had some very serious problems and an unpleasant history.

Many adopted children were born to unmarried parents. If this is true of your child, you may worry about how you should describe his beginnings to him. If you simply say, "Your birth mother wasn't married," you will be giving a straightforward, honest answer, yet you will not be condemning her. If this answer is not enough for him, he will ask you more.

When your child begins to express curiosity about his background and his heritage, let him know that this is a natural desire. Reassure him that there is no reason for him to feel hesitant or ashamed. Some experts feel that if adopted children knew more about their biological parents, they would feel less need to search for them.

Perhaps it is fear that makes adoptive parents feel insecure and uncomfortable about dealing with their child's background—fear that he will someday find his birth parents and like them better. An expression of interest by the child may be viewed by the adoptive parents as a sign of failure on their part or ingratitude on his part. In reality, the desire of many adopted teenagers and adults to learn about their heritage or to meet their birth parents usually arises out of a personal need, not out of failure on the part of the adoptive parents.

Adoptive parents usually want to know whether the adoption records can be legally opened. Most states have enacted laws to protect the confidentiality of everyone involved in an adoption. For all intents and purposes, adopted children are "reborn" into their adoptive families and have birth certificates to prove it. All traces of their beginnings are erased, leaving the child, the birth parents, and the adoptive parents free from ghosts out of the past. The best interest of the adoptee is the guiding principle for legal, administrative, and legislative decisions concerning adoptions.

Currently, however, some groups are putting increasing pressure on legislatures to allow adult adoptees to have free access to their adoption records. Whether this would be a good or a bad thing is open to discussion. On the one hand, it must be remembered that at the time of the adoption the birth parents and the adoptive parents were promised confidentiality. It is also possible that what would be revealed in those records would be quite disappointing or even harmful to the adoptee, especially if it led to a meeting with the birth parents. On the other hand, many people feel strongly that adults are capable of calculating the risks and should be allowed to make their own choices.

In spite of the confidentiality of the birth records, many adoptees find a good deal of information about their backgrounds. An adoptee's best initial source of information is his adoptive parents. In recent years many organizations have been established that offer adolescents or adults practical assistance in searching for background information or for birth parents.

Is such information, and the possibility of locating the birth parents, good or bad? There is no pat answer to this question. Whatever your opinion, you will be able to find studies, statistics, articles, and books to support it.

Many adoptees express concern as to whether their birth parents would want to see them. This is discussed at greater length in chapter 14. One teenager asked, "Why would they want me now if they didn't want me then?"

"If I ever do meet them, they would probably tell me to get lost," said another.

"I'm not bothered by the fact that my child wants to search for her roots," one adoptive father said. "That's natural. But it seems to me that for the good of everyone involved, this is an impulsive curiosity that should be controlled. We all have impulses that we must learn not to give in to—like punching someone in the mouth or telling a person to lay off the dessert because he's already too fat. But isn't maturity learning to control these impulses?"

"What makes parents of adopted kids think that all their

kids want to find their birth parents?" asked one sixteen-year-old boy. "My birth parents may be great people, but I don't want to meet them. I just want my real parents—the ones who raised me."

"There are some doors that should never be opened," said an adult adoptee, "because once they're opened, they're too difficult to shut. Sometimes they can never be shut again."

A social worker questioned, "Why are adoptive parents so afraid the biological parents are going to want their child back? That's less likely than being killed in an airplane crash. They have probably read too many romantic reports of ecstatic reunions. I'm sure they happen occasionally, but not nearly so often as we are led to believe. It's unrealistic to think that all those years can be just wiped out."

Nevertheless, there are instances when very disturbed, rebellious teenagers and young adults meet their birth mothers and immediately settle down to a normal life. Some adoptees, it seems, are unable to come to terms with who they are until they have had that contact with their beginnings. But this isn't always the case. It is important to distinguish between a real need to know and a form of quasi-searching in which an adolescent goes through a period of threatening his family with the the idea of searching for his birth parents. This is very much like other teenagers who threaten to run away from home. Adoptive parents, however, seem especially vulnerable to such threats; when they overreact, it appears to have the effect of reinforcing the power of the teenagers' threatenings.

"If I ever did meet my birth parents, it wouldn't change the way I feel," one teenager said. "My parents are my parents, and I'd never consider leaving them. They raised me and I love them."

There are a few adoptive parents who encourage and personally become involved in their children's search. One mother initiated it. At the beginning her son was mildly involved, but after several months he told her that he really wasn't interested. His mother continued the search alone. "The time will come when he will want to know," she said, "and when he does, I will have something to tell him."

As part of her search this mother attends the meetings of a local adoptees search organization. "I think all adoptive parents should become acquainted with one of these," she said. "They would get a completely different perspective of the adoptee's search."

"My daughter has lived with me for fourteen years," said another mother. "Her relationships with other people don't affect her relationship with me. That's already well established. Eventually she is going to have to live her own life. She has another set of parents and that concerns her. Because of this, I want her to find out as much as she can about it, and I will help her."

What is the answer? Most adoptive parents find that they have mixed feelings when they discover their child's interest in searching for his birth parents. Initially they may be hurt and angry. Usually, however, the relationship between the adoptive parents and their child is strong enough to withstand the strain of a search. The adoptive parents can provide vital emotional support at this time when one of the adoptee's greatest fears is that he will hurt the parents he loves.

Few adoptees get very far in their search, and even fewer ever make contact with their birth parents. In most cases a search proves disappointing. You and your child should be prepared for this. He will need your empathy and support in the face of this disappointment.

OPEN FORUM

RACHEL NICHOLS: *Our two children are very different. The younger one is full of questions, but the older one says little. She just doesn't seem to be interested. I guess it's a difference in their personalities.*

CHERYL KELLEY: *One of our children shows no interest at all in her birth mother or in any of the family records we have. But when she gets angry at her brothers and sister, she will say, "You're not really my family!" She obviously thinks more about it than she feels like sharing.*

MARIAN CRAWFORD: *Our older son is adopted, and the younger one was born to us. I worried all through my pregnancy that I would love my birth child more than my adopted one. Not long ago the older boy asked, "Mom, do you love me as much as my brother?" I could honestly and happily say, "Yes, I do." I'm telling the truth when I say that I feel no difference.*

LORRAINE SWANSON: *Our son's first question was, "Did I come from your tummy?" I said, "No, you came from someone else's tummy, but God made you just for us."*

PATRICK O'NEILL: *Our son said, "My birth mother must have really hated me. Why else would she have given me up?" What would be the best response to a question like that?*

RACHEL NICHOLS: *We encountered that same situation. It was hard for me to say, but I answered, "I don't know her reason for giving you up, but I know she must have loved you. It took love to allow you to be adopted into a home where you would be well cared for." I felt like adding, "But I'm a much better mother." Fortunately I resisted the temptation.*

DON COHEN: *We told our child that her birth mother surely loved her and that she would have kept her if she could have done so. It seems important to avoid denigrating the biological mother. Kids need to feel that they were born of essentially good and loving people and that they were not rejected because of who they are.*

RACHEL NICHOLS: *We got our girls when they were tiny babies. Their birth mothers could not have known them long enough to like or dislike them.*

MR. DONNELLY: *That's a good point. In many cases a birth mother who indicates that she plans to put her child up for adoption never even sees the baby.*

LORRAINE SWANSON: *Our child really was given up because he wasn't wanted. He had a birth defect that his parents just couldn't handle.*

KEN RANDLE: *You still could tell him that he was given up because his parents weren't able to care for him. Whether the reason was physical or emotional or whatever, the parents were unable to care for their child in all cases.*

JUDY RANDLE: *A psychologist we consulted warned us about some things not to say. "Your mother was too ill to care for you" may cause a child to worry whenever his adopted parents get sick, because he may fear that they won't be able to care for him either. "Your mother died" can cause the same kind of worry—that these parents will also die and leave him alone. He may even think that he caused his mother's death. If you say, "She was too poor to take care of you," he may get scared everytime he hears you complain about the high price of food. Or he may feel the need to search for his birth mother to take care of her.*

PATRICK O'NEILL: *Then what should we say?*

JUDY RANDLE: *The psychologist suggested that we merely say, "I don't know the reason, but it must have been a good one." In our case that's the whole truth. We really don't know.*

ROGER CRAWFORD: *Our son's parents were married, but they divorced when he was three, and his mother decided to give him up. They have since remarried and had two more children. The whole thing is a very bad situation involving drugs and crime. Without going into the details, we told him that they couldn't care for him.*

DR. MCDILL: *When children say such things as "My mother must have hated me," they may be voicing some specific feelings rather than inquiring about their birth mothers' reasons for allowing them to be adopted. I think I would approach the situation from the idea of what the child is feeling about himself. Is he uncomfortable? Is he unhappy about something? Is he feeling unworthy? What specific feelings brought this up? This may be more helpful than giving a cut-and-dried factual answer.*

KATHERINE O'NEILL: *I wish we hadn't been given so much information about our children's backgrounds. I can't see how it will ever do any good, and it really makes me feel uncomfortable having to wade through some direct questions when I would much rather be able to say truthfully, "I don't know."*

KEN RANDLE: *The older the children get, the more they want you to paint in the background of the birth mother. Sooner or later you're going to have to describe someone to fill in that shadow.*

JUDY RANDLE: *As our children got older and began to ask questions, we regretted the casual way we had dismissed and forgotten the information we were given at the time of the adoptions.*

BEN MEYERS: *Our social worker volunteered very little. We had to dig and pressure her for everything we got. But we figured, if we don't need it, fine; if we do, we'll have it.*

DR. MCDILL: *I agree. It's important to find out as much as possible about the ancestry and heredity of a child at the time of adoption rather than to say it doesn't matter and regret it later.*

BETSY VAUGHN: *Our attorney wrote comprehensive letters for both of our girls telling everything that was known about their backgrounds. When they began studying genealogy in school and were supposed to make out a family tree, it was really nice to have that letter.*

ROB ALVARADO: *One of our girls comes from an unbelievably sordid background involving drugs, crime, and prison. I'm afraid that such knowledge would be catastrophic to her self-image.*

DR. MCDILL: *You can only answer as honestly as you can, perhaps choosing to leave out the worst details.*

ROB ALVARADO: *I would have to lie in order to say anything good!*

JACK KELLEY: *Do you really think honesty would be so harmful?*

ROB ALVARADO: *Yes, I really do. And in time she'll surely ask. I guess I'll just have to make up something. A lie would be better than the truth.*

EVERYONE: *No! Don't lie!*

KEN RANDLE: *You're looking at this from a three-year-old's point of view. It will be a number of years before you actually have to deal with this problem. When your daughter is older, both you and she will be better able to handle it.*

ROGER CRAWFORD: *I'm in favor of giving a little bit of information over a long period of time, not piling it all on in one shocking session. Answer the little questions first, then add more as she asks and you feel that she's able to handle it.*

KEN RANDLE: *Sometimes we overreact and answer more than the child is asking.*

JACK KELLEY: *When she does ask, if you feel that your daughter is still too young, you could just say, "I don't think you're old enough to handle the answer right now. Ask me again next year, and if I feel that you're old enough, I'll tell you about it." An older child who really feels good about himself and has a secure family background can handle anything.*

ROB ALVARADO: *I don't know . . .*

JACK KELLEY: *Is there anything about your family background that, if you were told today, you couldn't handle?*

ROB ALVARADO: *No, I think I could handle anything. But I'm thirty-four years old. My daughter won't wait until she's my age to ask.*

JACK KELLEY: *By the time she's seventeen or eighteen, with the background you're giving her, she will do fine. I'm speaking from experience. Our oldest two are that age. They have been told the sordid details of their backgrounds and they have managed quite well.*

DR. MCDILL: *I want to stress again that moment of readiness. Don't try to explain what the child is not ready to hear. And, please,* don't *be dishonest! If the child later finds out that you lied to him, it will be far worse than whatever sordid details you may have avoided disclosing.*

JACK KELLEY: *What is it in the psychological makeup of a person that makes him so intent on finding those other parents?*

DR. MCDILL: *From a biblical standpoint, a separation accompanied by a very real sense of loss occurred at the time of the Fall. This inherent lostness, this forsakenness, is certainly a part of it. During adolescence a child begins to move away from identifying with his family and moves toward peer identification. He begins searching for an independent identity. For the adopted child, however, this search includes another set of parents. You mustn't feel threatened by this. It's completely normal. Your response should be, "I'm glad to see that you are growing up and getting your own ideas about things. I'm happy about that. Tell me about your feelings."*

GREG SWANSON: *This makes me awfully uncomfortable. How would the rest of you feel about your children undertaking a serious search for their birth parents?*

KAREN ALVARADO: *For the daughter who comes from such a terrible background I would be strongly against it. For the other one I would be more neutral.*

BETSY VAUGHN: *I'm dreading it for both our children. Neither one would be welcomed by her birth mother.*

MR. DONNELLY: *Children get an illusion of what their birth parents ought to be like. In virtually all cases, were they to see the reality, they would be extremely disappointed if not downright shocked.*

KATHERINE O'NEILL: *The family of our daughter's birth mother knows nothing about the child. If she should someday locate that mother and appear at her door, it would be a disaster. How can a birth mother ever make a new life for herself if she has to worry about that stranger stepping back into her life and breaking her heart?*

VICTORIA MEYERS: *I remember seeing in Ann Landers's column a letter that was written by a woman who had given up her child. She said that if her birth child ever reappeared, it would probably break up her marriage. If that happened, she said, she would sue everyone involved.*

BETSY VAUGHN: *The child must realize that the decision to adopt was made with everyone's best interests in mind. For fifteen or twenty years parent and child have gone their separate ways. That other person has a right to her new life.*

HOWARD VAUGHN: *Once that contact is made, no matter how it turns out, it can never be undone.*

DR. MCDILL: *I would recommend that any contact certainly be put off until adulthood. Dealing as an adult to an adult would be much better than dealing as a child to an adult.*

MR. DONNELLY: *Even the most radical groups pushing for the availability of birth records are opposed to making them available to anyone under eighteen.*

PATRICK O'NEILL: *An adult may well be satisfied simply to see the birth parents and not to push for actual contact. Someone less mature might be more likely to take it too far and cause real problems for himself or for his birth mother.*

DON COHEN: *Many people seem to be more interested in learning about their identities than they are in finding a new set of parents.*

JUDY RANDLE: *When our daughter was in college, she called our lawyer and asked him to find out all he could about her birth parents. He got some information together, but before he gave it to her he asked, "If we go through with this, if you even meet your birth mother, what do you think it will prove? Will you be happier? Will she?" After thinking it over, she told him that she had decided to forget the whole thing.*

JACK KELLEY: *Our children have a drastically different lifestyle than their other parents. They have very little in common.*

TERRY COHEN: *Our daughter has talked about wanting to meet her brother some day. She also says she wants to see what her mother looks like. She has this wild plan to find out where the woman lives and, as an encyclopedia saleswoman, to go knock on her door. I asked her what she thinks would happen if the woman were to open her door and see a carbon copy of herself standing there. She didn't give me an answer, but she must have thought about it, because she hasn't mentioned it again.*

CHERYL KELLEY: *Is it possible that the less the mystery surrounding those other people, the less the curiosity?*

DR. MCDILL: *I definitely think so. Mystery builds obsession. I would downplay the mystery in every way possible. Instead, the parents must encourage the building of a strong relationship between the child and the heavenly Father. This is the best life structure possible, and it will aid in the best possible development.*

ALLEN NICHOLS: *If we had thought that there was any chance of the adoption records' being opened, we would never have adopted in the first place. We were guaranteed total anonymity, and we feel that that promise must be honored.*

HOWARD VAUGHN: *What is the law? Can an adoptee get access to those birth records?*

MR. DONNELLY: *No, generally not except in the case of a dire need such as a medical condition. In a few states the laws are different in the case of independent adoptions. But these laws are currently under attack by many adoption-rights and right-to-know groups that are lobbying very intensely for new legislation. If laws on this do get passed, their constitutionality will be challenged. The right to privacy is a recognized constitutional right. The right of an adoptee to know his birth parents is not.*

BEN MEYERS: *If an attorney still knows the whereabouts of the birth mother, could an older adoptee ask him to communicate with her and ask if she would be interested in meeting?*

MR. DONNELLY: *Yes. A letter would be sent stating: "The other parties to the adoption would like to make contact. If you are interested, let me know. If I don't hear from you, I will assume that*

*you want to remain anonymous." That is clearly the way to proceed.
No one has the right to infringe upon the privacy of another.*

QUESTIONS FOR DISCUSSION

1. Do you think it's wise for a parent to initiate a search for his child's birth parents? Why or why not?
2. If your adopted child asked no questions about his background, what would you do?
3. Which situation discussed in this chapter would be the most difficult for you to handle? Why?

12. *Help!*

All parents worry about how their children will turn out, and that includes adoptive families. Because they love their children, parents want them to be happy. They also want to be able to look at them and feel a sense of satisfaction and pride.

As your child grows, you are bound to face problems with him. All parents do. Most will be normal, everyday problems of child rearing. But as an adoptive family you should be prepared to encounter more questions and more insecurity than others. Don't let this discourage you. Many authorities are quick to point out that there is a very high success rate among adoptive families who are willing to openly share their love, satisfaction, and pleasure as well as their frustrations, disappointments, and pain.

In some families disappointment, unhappiness, and frustration seem to be the predominent emotions. What are the problems that weigh them down? What can they do to help themselves? When they are no longer able to help themselves, to whom should they turn? In this chapter we seek answers to these difficult, sometimes painful questions.

THE INFLUENCE OF HEREDITY

"Our experience with adoption has been a painful disappointment," said a fifty-two year old woman. "If we had it to do again, we wouldn't adopt. It's too risky. A child inherits his behavior from his birth parents and there is nothing anyone can do about it."

No one will dispute the fact that an adopted child inherits a great deal biologically. Both adoptive parents may be short and heavy with dark brown hair. But if the child was born into a family of tall, thin, red-haired people, it will not take a genetics expert to tell us whom he will look like. An outgoing, athletic family may adopt a son who develops into a quiet, introspective poet. Your influence and encouragement will have a strong effect, but it won't make a football star of a person who has neither the talent nor the interest to play the game. Of course, such differences often occur in biological families as well.

All parents need flexibility and a willingness to accept their children's individuality, but adoptive parents especially so. It is unfortunate when people go into adoption with preconceived ideas of what their child will be like. Children have a way of surprising us. They seldom seem to turn out the way we picture them.

Adoptive parents must accept the fact that they will have limited knowledge of their child's heredity. This truth complicates their desire to understand and encourage the child's natural inclinations, to be aware of possible hereditary personality problems, and to be forwarned about inherited medical problems, including allergies, mental problems, diseases, and physical disorders.

"Most adoptive parents have higher-than-average intelligence," stated an adoptive father who is involved in counseling other adoptive parents. "But the majority of adopted kids come from just the opposite background. The environment in which they are raised will influence their development, but their inherited limitations will still be there. To be realistic, adoptive parents must recognize this."

Learning is a complex undertaking. Factors besides inborn intellect are physical and emotional well-being, the amount of support and encouragement received, and the child's temperament and attention span. Studies indicate that when children born to mentally inferior mothers were placed in their adoptive homes before the age of two, they reached educational, social, and occupational levels very much like their adoptive parents. While a child's innate ability sets an upper limit to what he can achieve, it is not the sole deciding factor.

Even so, there seems to be a disproportionately high percentage of learning problems among adoptees. Some claim that this is also true of behavior problems. Some adopted children fit into the categories that cause children to be labled "high risk" for learning and behavior problems without their adoptive parents even being aware of it. Children are considered high risk if—

- Their mothers had virus infections (such as measles) during the first three months of pregnancy;
- Their mothers had difficult and prolonged labor during birth;
- They were deprived of oxygen during birth;
- They are hyperactive;
- They were born to mothers who smoked and drank alcohol excessively during pregnancy;
- They were born to habitual drug users;
- They were born to mothers who had poor prenatal care;
- They were premature or post-term babies;
- They have severe allergies.

Just because a child displays one or more of these conditions, it does not necessarily mean that he will have learning or behavior problems. But if a child falls into the high-risk category, his parents should be aware of the possibility. If any problems do show up, early identification and treatment make a successful outcome much more likely.

Learning disabilities are the least recognized of all handicaps. A major federally funded research project found that 16 percent of all school children have some sort of learning disability. Although such children usually have a good, average, or above-average intellect they are unable to process what they see. This shows up as an inability to pay attention, to concentrate, to understand, to remember, or to properly control their activity. Children with such problems usually have trouble with reading, writing, or math. Because of their low tolerance for frustration and their inappropriate behavior, they are often considered simply "disciplinary problems." Frequently they are shunned and ridiculed by their peers.

Unless they receive professional help, these children seldom learn to live and work, to love and play as other children do. As they grow older, the inability of many of them to think logically compounds their problems. Typically, children with learning and behavior disabilities may drift in and out of contact with a variety of teachers, social workers, and school psychologists who are often unable to give them the help they need so badly. Some of the children grow up to lead fairly normal lives, but many others barely manage to scrape by. It is particularly sad that so many are never really able to develop their natural talents and abilities.

So what can adoptive parents do? They can become informed. They can keep in close touch with their children's progress in school. If they have reason to suspect a problem, they should have it checked out by the school psychologist or some other qualified professional. Accurate diagnosis and professional treatment are the most important remedies.

FACTORS BESIDES HEREDITY

What about traits and tendencies that are not commonly regarded as strictly biological? Can a child be genetically predisposed to alcoholism? To criminal behavior? To mental illness? I cannot give you these answers. Studies have been done but they present conflicting and inconclusive results. Even those professionals whose expertise is in this area are unable to agree on the relationship between heredity and other factors.

You can do nothing about your child's heredity, but you can do much to provide him with a positive, nurturing Christian environment. Concentrate on what you can do and trust God for the rest.

Perhaps the greatest challenge of parenthood is to help children to develop their unique potential and use it in the best ways possible. The temperament with which your child was born can be either a liability or an asset, depending on how it is developed and used. The strongest, most promising trait is the flipside of the weakest. The restless child has the same characteristic as the adult who, with boundless energy, keeps the Sunday school program running smoothly. The shy, introverted child can become that rarest of persons, the good listener. The frustratingly strong-willed child whose stubbornness drives you to distraction has the same temperament as the person you praise for having the strength of character and concentrated drives, to accomplish great things. What is most crucial is not a person's inborn temperament so much as the way in which that temperament is channeled.

There is a real danger in attributing your adopted child's

problems to his biological past and refusing to explore other possible causes. The specific genes that carry the master plan for any person can come from any combination of a host of distant, unknown, long-dead ancestors. There is no reason to assume that a child will be like his parents. We are all aware of cases where one child in a family of several stands out as strikingly different in appearance, temperament, or abilities.

By contrast, in many adoptive families there are remarkable instances of family likeness. People who live together tend to adopt one another's mannerisms and habits. To a certain extent, because of shared ideas and attitudes, people even grow to think and act alike.

Thus, even though heredity is important, it is the opinion of many professionals that the most significant influence on a child's future is the environment in which he is raised. The aims, examples, and daily training his parents give him will go a long way toward shaping the child into the person he will be as an adult. The best potential in the world will lead to nothing if it is not encouraged and developed.

Some of you will vigorously disagree on this issue. "We gave our adopted son every advantage," one father told me. "We were the very best parents we knew how to be. But that boy has been in trouble since he was thirteen. He is now twenty-two, and I see no sign of a change in him. Either he was genetically programmed for antisocial behavior, or my wife and I are terrible failures as parents."

Many families share this man's heartache, adoptive or not, Christian or not. Why is it that in a family of three children—sharing the same genetic background, home environment, and family expectations—there may be two loving kids and one who is an endless source of problems and hurt? Why is one child cooperative and conforming while his sibling is obstinate and rebellious? The fact is that God has made each of us responsible for what we do with life. Some people have great obstacles to overcome while others have seemingly endless advantages, but in the end each person bears the responsibility to decide what he will do with his life. Parents can train and pray and influence and teach, but the child himself does the choosing.

THE ROLE OF THE FATHER

One other issue is relevant to the problems relating to heredity and environment in the lives of adoptive children. That is the role of the father.

When a father gets involved in active fathering early in his child's life, both people benefit greatly. Researchers at Boston Children's Hospital Medical Center indicate that even very young babies behave differently with their fathers than they do with their mothers. They play gentle, cooing games with their mothers, but with their fathers they perk up and get ready for louder, more playful action. Michael Yogman, a pediatrician at the medical center, says, "Fathers have a unique role to play in their babies' lives—one that complements the mother's role." This holds true long past infancy.

Taking the responsibility of fathering seriously may mean that your priorities will need some rearranging. You may have to retrain yourself where emotional responses are concerned. Many men feel awkward and uncomfortable about showing love and affection to their children, especially their sons.

"I guess we men have never been taught to express our emotions as women have," said one father. "It's too bad. I think we've been cheated out of an awful lot!"

Most adoptive fathers take their role of fathering very seriously. Maybe the reason is that they want and prepare for fatherhood during the adoption process in ways that natural fathers might not. They have had to endure disappointment and waiting. They have been carefully screened to ensure that they are well suited and qualified. One adoptive father said, "Most any man can be a father, but it takes a really special one to be a daddy."

As a father, are you loving, affectionate, responsive, involved, available, and approachable? Or distant, aloof, and always busy? Do you consider parenting to be primarily a mother's task? If your view of fathering is limited to a game of baseball with the children on Saturday and taking the family on a two-week vacation in the summer, you are missing out on a great deal. So is your child.

It has been said that there is a definite correlation between a person's view of God and his relationship with his father. The modeling done by a father can influence his children in basic spiritual concepts and the attitude of faith. This is largely implicit, not explicit instruction; it is powerful, for good or ill. Fathering is serious business with eternal implications.

THE HYPERACTIVE CHILD

Adoptive parents are concerned with many other issues that, while not having eternal significance, can have momentous consequences. We do well to consider some of these. The first is hyperactivity.

"One of our daughters is hyperactive," said one mother. "She's so easily distracted that she has a hard time concentrating and consequently doesn't do well in school. Isn't this a fairly common problem among adopted children?"

It seems to be. Of all the challenges parents can face, few are more demanding and frustrating than hyperactivity. Its severity can range from a child with a very short attention span to a child who is totally out of control.

Special behaviors generally associated with hyperactivity are impulsiveness, constant activity, being overdemanding, social immaturity, frequent crying, temper tantrums, unpredictability, destructiveness, stubbornness, irritability, defiance, a short attention span, aggressiveness, disruptive behavior, inability to follow directions, failure to respond to discipline, and inability to tolerate cuddling. Fortunately no hyperactive child will have all these symptoms, and many children who are not hyperactive will show one or more of them. But if your child expresses several of these behavior patterns continually, it is wise to look into the matter. Be aware that a true diagnosis of hyperactivity must be made by a trained professional. You should not take your next door neighbor's word for it, and you should not make the diagnosis yourself.

Often the parents of a hyperactive child will be made to feel guilty for her problems. A growing number of professionals now believe that the vast majority of instances of hyperactivity are the result of innate differences in temperament and not the fault of the parents. How the child is raised can either complicate or ease the problem, but it is unlikely that upbringing is the cause.

What can you do if you suspect that your child is

hyperactive? First get a sound, professional diagnosis. Have your child tested by a pediatrician whom you know to be knowledgeable about hyperactivity. Once you are satisfied as to the diagnosis, learn all you can about this disability. Two excellent books on this subject are *The Hyperactive Child* by Paul Wender, M.D., and *Why Your Child Is Hyperactive* by Ben Feingold, M.D. (see appendix 3).

Because a hyperactive child is often confused by an overstimulating environment, it is a good idea to put away extra toys, especially those that frustrate her. Also try to simplify daily tasks that seem to cause her trouble.

Other people are likely to be part of your problem. Don't expect too much from them. They don't understand hyperactivity as you do, and they don't know your child. Explain your child's problem to them and let them know how they can help. This is especially important in the case of Sunday school teachers, baby-sitters, and other people who will be working with your child regularly.

Consistent discipline is essential. Setting firm and fair rules is paramount. When your child breaks the rules, follow through with an appropriate punishment. Hyperactive children need a carefully structured environment.

Be positive and affectionate in your handling of your child. Make an effort to talk softly. Hug her. Caress her. Hold her. But temper your positive attitude with realism. Your child will place great demands on you. Coping with his boundless, often misdirected energy will often leave you tired, frustrated, and angry. There will be times when you feel totally inadequate or guilty. You may feel like a dismal failure. When this happens, acknowledge your feelings; they are normal. Denying your negative feelings will only lead to more problems.

Always work toward helping your child to develop his potential. Build his self-confidence. Help him to develop ways to compensate for his weaknesses. Show him by your attitude, words, and actions that you truly believe that God knows the answers and that He does all things well. With God's help, there is no situation you can't handle.

ADOLESCENCE

Your greatest challenges in parenthood will come during your children's adolescence. In our complex world adolescence is a time of turmoil and confusion in the struggle for a personal identity. Natural children may be at a loss to explain their parents' "unfair behavior." Adopted children think they have an explanation: they reason that they are living with strangers. What a perfect excuse for explaining every problem. Somehow, though, that doesn't acknowledge that their nonadopted friends are experiencing the exact same trials.

"My mother won't let me do anything!" a fifteen-year-old girl complained. "She doesn't trust me at all. She doesn't even try to understand me. I think it would be different if she were my *real* mother—if I had been born to her."

The adolescent has a need to gain her independence. Because it is important that she establish herself as an individual separate from her family, it is almost inevitable that problems will arise during this transition from childhood to adulthood.

A teenager's need to know about herself often becomes intertwined with her normal rebelliousness and desire for independence. Her mind is not always open to logic or to facts, especially if they don't agree with her feelings.

The greatest quest of the teenage years seems to be the search to "find oneself." Questions from your child about her background are inevitable. For the adopted teenager this raises questions that can be nearly impossible to answer. Very likely only limited information will be available to her, and that may just serve to make her more curious than ever. An unknown factor about the past cannot easily be incorporated into a sense of self, so many adopted teenagers feel a need to search for their biological parents. Adolescence, however, is no time to begin such a search. But it is a good time to reassure your child that it was not through any fault of hers that she was released for adoption. Teenagers need reassurances of their own worth.

SELF-ESTEEM

A big problem for many people is low self-esteem. We are so precious and worthwhile to God that He was willing to sacrifice His own Son to redeem us. Yet we persist in thinking of ourselves as inferior, never quite measuring up to everyone else. Children have this problem, too, and adolescents most of all. Since they have to deal with the fact that they were once rejected, it is not surprising that adoptees seem to be especially vulnerable to feelings of self-doubt.

The problem of low self-esteem is due in part to the society in which we live. For us a person's worth is measured against idealistic standards of physical attractiveness, athletic prowess, high intelligence, and social acceptability. These standards are artificial and foolish. We all know that. Still, to be honest we have to admit that to some extent all of us are affected by them.

What can you do to help your adopted child develop a healthy self-concept? This is a complex problem, but the following five points may prove helpful:

- *Examine the values you are fostering in your home.* Whether we like it or not, we are all products of our society. We want beautiful, smart, popular kids just as much as the next person. But you must be completely accepting of your child even if he is somewhat less than perfect.
- *Treat your child wisely.* He deserves your unconditional love. His positive points should be reinforced with sincere, spontaneous praise. And be especially careful about what kind of joking and teasing goes on in you home. Never poke fun at anyone's weak spots. If anything intended as play is disturbing to the child, end it at once.
- *Help your child to compensate for his weaknesses.* It is not possible to remove all your child's obstacles or to shield him from every hurt. It is foolish even to try. But you can help him to discover his strengths and to make the most of them while deemphasizing his weaknesses.
- *Encourage your child to assume responsibility and independence.* This will naturally be progressive. As your child matures and proves his dependability, he should be rewarded with increased responsibility and independence.
- *Discipline wisely.* If you do not discipline your child at all, it will increase his feelings of not belonging and not

really being loved. Overpermissiveness can create feelings of insecurity. By contrast, inconsistent or cruel punishment can permanently damage his self-image. Just what are the elements of wise discipline? First, establish the rules in advance. Second, be consistent; a broken rule should *always* mean punishment. Third, the child should not be punished for mistakes or accidents. Fourth, after punishment has been meted out, reassure your child that you still love him just as much as ever. Fifth, be sure that the punishment fits both the infraction and the child's age.

If you are successful in developing a healthy self-concept in your child, you have given him a priceless treasure. You have given him the armor to protect himself from the bumps and bruises of life.

OPEN FORUM

ROB ALVARADO: *I blame TV programs and movies for a lot of the misconceptions concerning adoption. I really resent the way they misrepresent adopted families and their problems.*

CHERYL KELLEY: *So do I! The TV show I dislike the most is* The Brady Bunch. *At the height of its popularity people would tell us how much our family was like the Brady family. What a laugh! Anyone who has ever spent an hour in our home knows that the only possible similarity is that we're both blended families with a houseful of kids.*

BETSY VAUGHN: *To me, the most disturbing stories are the ones that describe sentimental accounts of adult adoptees who are reunited with their birth parents. You see such stories on television, in the newspapers, and in magazines. They are presented in a sensational manner and are misleading. Kids get the idea that every woman who ever gave up her baby for adoption is anxiously awaiting his reappearance.*

JACK KELLEY: *Even when children are raised in a happy, secure home and are well-adjusted, there seems to come a time when they just need to know about their biological parents. At least that is how it has happened in our family.*

DON COHEN: *When our daughter was first adopted, I wrote out a letter telling her what it meant to us to have her come into our family. I told her how strongly we felt that God had sent her to us and how we had all planned and prepared for her arrival. I included everything I knew about her parents, her background, the details of the common-law marriage of her parents, and even about her father's desertion of the family. I also told her about her only natural sibling, a brother three years older than she. I emphasized that giving her up had been a hard but loving decision on her mother's part. We put the letter away with instructions that in the event of our deaths it was to be given to her. Otherwise we would give it to her when we felt that she needed to know that information.*

TERRY COHEN: *It hurts to admit it, but Don and I have been disappointed in our adopted daughter. It is possible that we have been guilty of setting unrealistically high expectations for her, but I just wonder if some of her behavior problems are due to poor heredity. There are more and more people today who feel that all of us are more a product of our heredity than of our environment. As adoptive parents we must at least consider this possibility.*

JACK KELLEY: *I can't accept that. We have seen fantastic personality and attitude changes in our children even though some of them were older when we all came together. We attribute the changes to the working of the Lord in their lives.*

HOWARD VAUGHN: *Our girls don't look different from the other children, but both of them have problems with self-esteem. I think it's because their school classmates make demeaning remarks to them and let them know that they are considered second-class because they are adopted. I'm afraid that they are in for a pretty rough life if we can't do something about their low self-esteem.*

BETSY VAUGHN: *They tend to be controlled by what their friends think. But we can't always choose their friends for them, especially now that they are getting older.*

DR. MCDILL: *I deal a lot with problems of self-esteem. It's really quite a complex problem. You cannot merely bolster your children up with compliments. What you say will not agree with their feelings, and it is their feelings that they will believe. Instead, you need to let them know that you have confidence in their ability to think and to reason out the facts. By asking, "What do you think about this?" or*

143

"What would you do in a case like that?" you will be demonstrating your confidence in their judgment. They will begin to think, "Hey, they really do want my opinion!" When they know that you have confidence in them, they will begin to have confidence in themselves.

HOWARD VAUGHN: *That's good. We have been trying to pump them up with compliments, but it has not worked.*

DR. MCDILL: *No, because their self-esteem has nothing to do with your opinion of them—it is what they think of themselves. There are many other factors involved, of course, but this is basic.*

GREG SWANSON: *Does the whole "roots" thing have anything to do with a person's self-concept?*

DR. MCDILL: *Yes, it does. We all have innate feelings of wanting to belong. We all try to find a historic root with which we can identify. I think this is at the bottom of the typical teenage quest to "find himself."*

TERRY COHEN: *Our daughter, the youngest of our three children and the only one who is adopted, was a real joy to us until she reached adolescence. Suddenly she was a different person—angry, resentful, and rebellious. Her greatest desire seemed to be to hurt and embarrass us. She has purposely sought out friends of whom we were sure to disapprove.*

DON COHEN: *She has been more hurtful to her mother than to me. The girl will hardly speak to Terry or allow her to touch her.*

TERRY COHEN: *Two years ago, when she was eighteen, our daughter began to pressure us about finding her birth parents. We felt it was time to give her the letter Don had written when we first got her, since it contained all the information we had. When she read it, it really seemed to help. I'm sure it was the Lord's timing.*

JUDY RANDLE: *Do you blame adoption for your daughter's problems?*

TERRY COHEN: *Yes, I do.*

JUDY RANDLE: *That's interesting, because Ken and I have a strikingly similar situation in our family, but with a slightly different twist. We also have three children—two adopted, the middle one born to us. It is our child by birth who has been our big problem. At nineteen she shows no sign of changing her attitude.*

DON COHEN: *I guess in the end we parents can only give our children over to the Lord's keeping and prayerfully wait for a change in their behavior.*

SEEKING OUTSIDE HELP

There are times when problems arise that are too big for parents to handle. In a time of crisis, what can they do? Where should they turn?

"Often I was at my wit's end with Tad," said the mother of a boy adopted at the age of ten. "One morning I was ready to turn him over to the welfare department or to anyone else daring enough to take him. I cried and I prayed and I cried some more. Believe me, it's terrible to feel like a total failure as a parent! In desperation I called an acquaintance who had gone through problems with her own adopted son. She told me about a support group that had helped her. My husband and I started attending, and it made all the difference in the world."

"We had problems, real problems," one father said. "What we did was to find another Christian family who were going through the same things we were. Sharing with them was an enormous help to us. By talking and praying together we both became stronger. We really needed to know that there was someone who truly understood our pain. It's important for Christian parents to unite so that they can support and encourage each other when these problems erupt."

Self-help groups prove to be lifesavers for many adoptive parents. They can share tips and experiences and receive front-line help from people who have been there. Sometimes just knowing that you are not alone, that your problems are not unique, is enough to enable you to cope with the situation you are facing.

How do you go about finding a support group? Your local adoption agency is probably your best contact; they will often be able to refer you to a group. Your minister might be able to put you in touch with people who are in a similar situation.

If you have reason to believe that the problems your child is experiencing are too serious to be handled by such a group, it is time to find an experienced counselor. It is possible that the professional will only need to assure you that your child's

145

behavior is indeed normal and that you have no reason to worry. Nevertheless, if there really is a problem, a trained, experienced professional is the one who should help.

How do we find the right professional? Again, your local adoption agency is a good source of advice. Most agencies will offer counseling to families who need it even if the child was not adopted through them. Another possibility is to get referrals from several people who have had dealings with psychologists, psychiatrists, or family counselors and have been pleased with them. Ministers may be able to recommend professional counselors also.

Is it important to insist on a Christian counselor? Without a doubt a trained, competent, experienced Christian should be the counselor of choice. You would both be building on the same foundation. You would be able to base your quest for an answer on sound, biblical principles. A Christian counselor has resources that the non-Christian knows nothing about. He can draw on the guidance of the Holy Spirit and share the unconditional, unending love of God. You will be able to pray and talk together in a way that would not be possible with someone who does not share your relationship with Christ.

This is the ideal. But it is not always possible to find a trained, competent Christian counselor. In this case it is better to work with a non-Christian who knows what she is doing than to work with a Christian who has no training or experience. But whether or not the counselor is a Christian, it is vitally important that she share your basic values.

In the end you must accept your child for what he is. Let him know that there is nothing he can do that will make you stop loving him. God is loving and forgiving, and He has unlimited patience. You must try to demonstrate the same qualities. With God's help you can.

For reasons we cannot understand, God sometimes chooses to allow Christian parents to suffer through the actions of their children. When we see nothing but our hopeless problems, when we groan under the weight of our pain, it is reassuring to know that God has the answers. He knows the reasons. When we are forced to acknowledge our helplessness, we must lovingly let our children go and trust them to the safekeeping of God. We can only pray that they will be brought to the point where they themselves will make the decision to come to Him.

OPEN FORUM

KEN RANDLE: *I am sure that there never was a parent who wasn't periodically faced with problems. Children can't get their growing done without going through stages, and some of them can be very irritating and upsetting. Parents should learn all they can about child development so that they will be better prepared to understand and to accept the different kinds of behavior they see in their children.*

ROGER CRAWFORD: *Every parent, by birth or adoption, runs the risk of having a rebellious or difficult child.*

DR. MCDILL: *In my opinion, it's a mistake to regard adoption itself as a source of probable difficulty. That's not to say, however, that adopted children don't have certain areas of increased vulnerability.*

CHERYL KELLEY: *I think it is harder to raise an adopted child than a biological one. The rewards are just as great, but the periods of failure seem to hit a lot harder.*

LORRAINE SWANSON: *The most painful adoption-related problem for us is the negative attitudes of our relatives. It isn't only what they say; often it is what they leave unsaid or what they say by their actions. We were aware of their feelings from the beginning, but we were afraid that if we put any pressure on them, they might completely break off their relationship with us. We decided that we could deal with their attitude more easily than we could deal with a brick wall between us.*

GREG SWANSON: *As they got to know our son, their negative attitude softened a little. But it did not disappear. We have learned to accept it and to live with it.*

DR. MCDILL: *How does your son react?*

LORRAINE SWANSON: *He's only six. He doesn't seem to notice.*

RACHEL NICHOLS: *How do you react when your child comes home from school and out of the blue says, "You're not my real mother!"*

MARIAN CRAWFORD: *He was probably just needling you. That's happened to me. Once when I gave my son canned spaghetti for lunch he announced, "I don't like spaghetti and I won't eat it and*

147

you can't make me, because you're not my mother!" I said, "Well, since I'm not your mother I guess I don't need to fix you anything else." When he got really hungry he came back and sheepishly said, "Uh, Mommy . . ."

ROB ALVARADO: *It's not unusual for a child, biological or adopted, to say, "I hate you!" If you let a comment like that get to you, the child will use it again and again. He is just looking for a button to push.*

ROGER CRAWFORD: *Another possibility is that he is asking, "How can you be my mother if I wasn't born to you?"*

KATHERINE O'NEILL: *When our daughter said, "You aren't my real mother," I acknowledged the fact that I had not given birth to her. But I added that I was the one who did the loving and the caring, the one who was raising her. So I agreed in part, but I pointed out the difference.*

MARIAN CRAWFORD: *We are our children's real parents in every sense except the biological one, and that's what we want them to understand.*

ALLEN NICHOLS: *Before we can convince* them, *we must first convince* ourselves.

MR. DONNELLY: *People often come to me and say, "When you talk to the* real *mother, . . ." and I say, "Wait a minute! Nine months does not a real mother make."*

TERRY COHEN: *Real parents are the people who care for a child, comfort him and soothe him, feed him and play with him, take him to school, and sit up all night with him when he's sick. Biological or adoptive, all parents have to grow to be real parents through their daily loving care of the child.*

DON COHEN: *It is being loved and cared for that makes a family. The experiences shared day by day bind them together and help the child to understand what it is to be part of a family.*

ALLEN NICHOLS: *Whether you are born into a family or adopted into it, once you are there you are a real part of that family. I feel that I have a greater understanding and appreciation of God's love for me because of the love I feel for my children.*

DON COHEN: *We consider our adopted daughter to be a chosen child, but not chosen by us. God chose us to be her parents. We didn't have a choice in our natural children, and we didn't have a choice in her either.*

TERRY COHEN: *We explained our daughter's place in the family to her by telling her, "Mommy and Daddy came by marrying each other, the other children came by birth, and you came by adoption. How we came into the family isn't important. What is important is that we are all together just as God planned it."*

ROB ALVARADO: *I dislike the term "real mother."*

CHERYL KELLEY: *When our children were younger, the littlest one said something about her "real" mother. The oldest boy turned to me and said, "What are you, Mom? Our plastic mother?"*

RACHEL NICHOLS: *What would be a better designation than "real" mother?*

TERRY COHEN: *The current term of choice seems to be "biological" mother.*

GREG SWANSON: *That's O.K. for us, but a little child couldn't say that.*

BETSY VAUGHN: *I don't like "natural" mother because that makes me feel like an unnatural mother.*

ALLEN NICHOLS: *Not necessarily. Maybe you're a supernatural mother.*

KATHERINE O'NEILL: *I have heard "your other mother" used, but I don't like that because it seems to indicate that the first parents are still available somewhere. It makes them seem as real and as vital to our children as Patrick and I are.*

ROB ALVARADO: *I like "birth mother." It is easy to say, and it gets the true picture across.*

MARIAN CRAWFORD: *Several times my son has said things like "My real mother would understand." That can be upsetting when I hear it too often or at the wrong times.*

JUDY RANDLE: *Once I overheard my daughter and her friend talking in the next room. The friend said, "She's not your real mother. You're adopted." I loved my daughter's answer. She said, "So what if I'm adopted? She is still my real mother."*

149

QUESTIONS FOR DISCUSSION

1. Under what circumstances should you seek out a professional counselor?
2. Can you think of other ways to locate a good counselor in your area?
3. Which problem in this chapter would be the most difficult for you to handle? Do you have any further suggestions toward a solution for that problem?

13.

No Longer My Child

"It has been more than thirty years," Claudia Greenley, a tiny gray-haired grandmother, said quietly. "Why is it that I still can't talk about David without tears? It was such a terribly painful experience that even after all this time the hurting still hasn't stopped. I don't suppose it ever will."

People love to tell success stories of their experiences with adoption and of the great joy their children have brought into their lives. Many inspiring books have been written about families who have adopted several little ones, sometimes with great physical or mental handicaps. Overcoming great odds, these people have been able to weld the children together into a happy, healthy, loving family. The message seems to be "With enough faith and enough love, you too can overcome any problems." But there are families whose adoption experiences have ended with dashed dreams and broken hearts. Their stories are seldom told.

Fortunately the percentage of unsuccessful adoptions is quite small. When failures do occur, they are generally confined to cases involving handicapped or older children—the ones who are most likely to bring deep-rooted problems into their new homes.

"Both my daughter Elizabeth and I were lucky to have survived her long and difficult birth," Claudia Greenley said. "The doctor told me that I must never risk another pregnancy. I was more than disappointed—I was absolutely devastated! Henry and I had always planned on having five or six stairstep children, and I just couldn't adjust my thinking to raising our little girl alone.

"When Elizabeth was two years old, Henry and I decided that we could still have our big family. We would adopt. In those days there were many babies available. But Henry was in

151

the army, and we were moved around so often that we were never able to meet the agencies' residency requirements.

"Finally, after four years of frustration, I went to an adoption agency in the area to which we had just moved and literally begged them to give me a child. I was told that if we would be willing to take an older child, one could be placed with us immediately. I went home and talked it over with Henry. Since Elizabeth was now six years old, we figured that an older child would fit in just fine. I knew how much Henry would enjoy a son—he loves camping and fishing and all kinds of sports—so at my suggestion we requested an older boy.

"David arrived the very next week. He descended upon our quiet, well-ordered home with all the grace of a hurricane. He was ten years old and small for his age, but awfully strong. He was endlessly energetic and unbelievably loud. We all stared in wonder at this strange boy who roared in and took over our home."

"In his own eyes," Henry Greenley interjected, "David was the greatest. He thought he deserved the best of everything. When we went out to dinner, which we enjoyed doing often, he always ordered the most expensive meal on the menu. When other boys came to play, the whole neighborhood could hear David bossing them around. And school was a problem from the very beginning. David was a terrible bully, always getting into fights. He did very little school work. I knew I had to discipline him, but whenever I did, he would scream and swear at me, then stomp off to his room to pout. David surely didn't fit my idea of what a son should be."

"But he was good to Elizabeth," Claudia added quickly. "She loved him dearly and followed him everywhere, just like a puppy. David was always gentle with her. He really did love his little sister."

"If he truly cared about Elizabeth," Henry said, "she was the only one who ever got through to him. To everyone else he was nothing but trouble."

"I tried so hard to love him," Claudia said, "but he really made it hard. Whenever he didn't get his way he would yell, 'You don't love me! I'm going to run away!' That scared me so much that I did everything I could to meet his demands. In an effort to prove our love we bought David all the expensive toys that were so important to him, even though it was a real financial hardship for us. But then he shocked us by systematically destroying every single toy! One time he traded an expensive electric train for a baseball mitt and a pocketknife. Then he used the knife to slash the mitt to pieces. He really scared me when he did things like that.

"The stress David put on our family started to cause problems between Henry and me. We could see that our family was in trouble, but we didn't know where to turn for help. We weren't Christians at the time and we did not attend church, so we had no minister to counsel with us. We called David's caseworker at the adoption agency, but she just shrugged off our problems and told us to be patient and to give David more time and more love."

"That was a laugh!" Henry said bitterly. "By that time any love I ever felt for David was long gone."

"The breaking point came when Henry told me that unless David was gone by the end of the week, he would take Elizabeth and move out," Claudia said. "I felt terrible about returning David to the agency, but what could I do? I admit that once I was forced to make the decision, however, I felt better than I had since the day David arrived. It was as if the weight of the world had suddenly been lifted from my shoulders.

"Still, you cannot imagine the guilt I've carried all these years. I'm certain that David was never adopted again. I just can't help but think that we might have been able to work things out if only we had been given some help." She paused. "But maybe I'm wrong. Maybe nothing could have helped us."

COMPETENT COUNSELING

The Greenleys' story points up the absolute necessity of competent, sympathetic counselors who are readily available when problems first become evident. Today most adoption agencies are willing and able to provide this assistance. Other sources of help include ministers, physicians, school personnel and the local department of mental health. While a Christian counselor may be preferable, God can work through a non-Christian. In either case it is essential that the person be a competent, qualified professional who shares your philosophy of

153

life. Had the Greenleys had access to such a person, perhaps they could have come to understand the causes of David's actions. Perhaps they could have learned to help him to trust and to love. Perhaps, despite all the problems, they could have found a permanent place for him in their family.

"When we adopted David," said Claudia Greenley, "we had no concept of God's guidance in such a personal matter, so the idea of asking Him for help never occurred to us. We had been unfortunate enough to have gotten a very troubled child. It was embarrassing and frustrating to be unable to handle David, and we were ashamed to have failed so miserably. Had we been Christians, had we entered into the adoption with prayer and with some sense of divine guidance, maybe then things would have turned out differently."

Maybe, but not necessarily. From the very beginning the adoption of twelve-year-old Patty by Peter and Carol Ann Messina was surrounded by prayer.

"From the time I first saw Patty," Carol Ann said, "I realized that she was a fascinatingly complex person. She's a beautiful girl with a sweet nature. She is also loud and boisterous and at times can be annoying. She moved into a foster home in our neighborhood and was immediately befriended by our two daughters, who were ten and fourteen at the time.

"Patty had spent most of her life in foster homes—she couldn't even remember how many. One day when she was swimming in our backyard pool, I overheard her talking to my younger daughter. 'You sure are lucky to have a real home,' she said. 'I get moved around so much that I don't even unpack my clothes anymore.' My heart went out to that poor girl. Can you imagine a child growing up homeless and unwanted?

"When summer came, Patty was at our house constantly. She really was a dear, but she also had some irritating habits. I didn't realize how often I was making such remarks as, 'If Patty were *my* child, I would . . .' until my younger daughter finally retorted, 'If you think you could help Patty so much, why don't we just adopt her? She's at our house all the time anyway, and no one else wants her.'

"My daughter's comment and my mothering instinct set us all to thinking. Perhaps God had brought Patty into our lives because He wanted her to be a permanent part of our family.

We had all been praying for Patty for quite a while, but now our prayers changed. We started asking God for clear, definite direction. If He wanted Patty to join our family, and if He would be in the union, we asked that He open a way for us to adopt her. We also asked that He give us a sign to assure us that we were doing the right thing. If the adoption was not His will, we prayed that the doors would be unmistakably closed.

"With the opening of school that fall, Patty was around less frequently. Still she came over almost every evening to have our girls help her with her homework. She had always been a poor student in school, Patty told us. It was obvious that her personal study skills were nonexistent. But we were quite impressed at the effort she seemed to be making.

"Then one morning during the week before Thanksgiving, Patty burst into our house at seven-thirty. Though it was almost impossible to understand her through her sobs, we were finally able to gather that her foster father had taken a job in another city and the family would soon be moving away. Patty was to be moved to still another foster home. Sinking into a kitchen chair, she buried her face in her hands and wept. 'You're my best friends in the whole world,' she cried. 'Now I won't ever see you again!'

"How my heart ached for that little girl! She looked so small and helpless and vulnerable. Without taking the time to think it through, I blurted, 'Maybe you could stay here with us.' Patty stared at me in disbelief. So did everyone else. Surely this was our sign from the Lord. He was assuring us that He did want Patty to be with us. That very week the arrangements were made."

"When Patty came into our family she had never been exposed to spiritual things," said Peter Messina. "She had no spiritual awareness at all and very little interest. But once she began attending church with us and got to know the other kids in Sunday school and the youth group, she seemed to enjoy it and to fit right in. It was hard for her to sit through the church service, but then I guess that's understandable. Though she never actually protested, she fidgeted and wiggled and checked my watch a lot. Even so, she apparently heard and understood a lot more than we realized. She was never one to share her thoughts with us, but she would occasionally ask me questions

155

like 'Does God love me too?' and 'How do you know God is real?' and 'Can anyone who wants to, be God's child?'

"I answered her questions as honestly as I could, trying to encourage her without being pushy. Our daughters were a great help. Their faith is sincere and matter-of-fact, and Patty was open to anything that came from them."

"Patty was always rather cold and distant to me," Carol said. "She rejected every effort I made to hug or kiss her. I was sure that with enough motherly love I could win her over, but the more affectionate I was to her, the more difficult the situation became. Before long Patty became openly rude and disrespectful to me. That was especially hard for me to handle because she was so open and loving to Peter and the girls. What was I doing wrong? I tried everything I could think of to improve our relationship, but nothing helped. It was the most frustrating, most exasperating experience of my life.

"When the friction continued to increase, Peter took Patty to see a psychiatrist suggested by her school counselor. After a few sessions he assured Peter that physically Patty was a healthy, alert, intelligent girl. But he also said that she was deeply troubled. Having been cruelly and painfully abused and rejected by her birth mother, Patty was placed in a foster home. There she was further abused by her foster mother. Because of these painful experiences, Patty had developed a deep distrust—almost a hatred—for women. Though she badly needed love and security, she had long ago learned not to expect much from an adult, especially one who calls herself 'mother.' For me ever to establish any kind of a positive relationship with Patty, I would need an endless supply of patience and a boundless reserve of love. Even then, any hope of a real mother-daughter love developing between us was probably unrealistic.

"I can't tell you my dismay at hearing the psychiatrist's report. My mind was flooded with questions. Could I possibly raise a child under such circumstances? Could I give Patty all the patience and love she needed? Were we making a mistake by adopting a child with such problems? I had no answers, so I took the situation directly to the Lord. First I reminded God that neither Peter nor I had ever searched out a child to adopt; it was He who had brought Patty to us. Then I reminded Him that from the very beginning our whole family had sincerely prayed for His will and His guidance in this matter. I reminded Him, too, that to the best of our ability Peter and I were following His leading. So why, I demanded, was everything turning out bad?

"Soon difficulties began to arise between our girls and Patty. Although she was twelve years old, Patty was so irresponsible and unpredictable that we dared not leave her without adult supervision even for a short time. That meant that either we had to restrict our own daughters' privileges to match the limited ones we were able to give Patty, or else we had to listen to Patty's accusations that we were showing partiality to our own girls. We finally settled on an uneasy compromise: sometimes we restricted the other girls' freedom, and at other times we maintained a different set of rules for them than for Patty. The results were terrible. Our girls resented Patty, and Patty resented them.

"Academics also became a problem. Our girls have always been excellent, motivated students. Patty was just the opposite. We tried hard to avoid comparisons, but Patty felt hopelessly outclassed by her straight-A sisters."

"Soon after Patty moved in with us," said Peter, "I was awarded a contract on which I had been working for almost a year. The only problem was that I would have to be out of the state for the next few months. This couldn't have come at a worse time. Carol Ann was having real problems with Patty, and the girls were complaining about her more every day. It seemed that I was the only one to whom Patty could relate. I almost decided to turn down the contract, but then I reasoned that with my being absent from the situation at home, perhaps Patty would be drawn closer to Carol Ann. It didn't work out that way."

"Those four months were the most miserable time of my entire life!" exclaimed Carol Ann. "I had absolutely no control over Patty; she just ran wild. I scolded and I punished. I even tried the positive approach. Cookie baking is a favorite activity at our house, so I would tell Patty, 'If you do your jobs quickly, you can help me make cookies.' That child would respond by walking slowly to her room, sitting down on the bed, and refusing to do a single thing. I'm sure it was that she just didn't want to be involved in any activity that included me. That really

157

hurt. It also angered and frustrated me. No matter how hard I tried, I could not win that girl over.

"More and more I resented the time and attention I was wasting on Patty. She took so much out of me that I was unjustly sharp and impatient with the other girls. It just wasn't fair to them or to me. Every morning I would wake up promising myself that I wouldn't allow anything to upset me that day. Whatever was done, whatever was said, I would take it all in stride. But before the girls were even off to school, I would be angry and someone would end up in tears."

"When I returned home after my four-month absence, I couldn't believe the situation I found awaiting me," Peter said. "I could hardly recognize my formerly happy, loving, cheerful family. Now everyone was moody and touchy. One night after Carol Ann and I had gone to bed, our two daughters tiptoed into our bedroom and locked the door behind them. Lying down on our bed, they burst into tears. We hugged them close and soon we were crying too. The older girl sobbed, 'Remember how happy our family used to be? Please, please, can't we be like that again?'

"We remembered the events that had brought us to the adoption. We recalled all the prayers and good intentions that had gone into it. Then Carol Ann suggested that we pray about it. And we did pray, the four of us together, long into the night. The more we prayed, the more certain we became that for the good of our family, Patty would have to go.

"I called the agency the next morning while the girls were at school," Carol Ann said. "That evening we all gathered by the fireplace in the living room and we told Patty of our decision. Peter explained that we just couldn't be the family she needed. Patty asked if we liked her; we said we did. She asked where she would go next; we said we didn't know, but wherever it was, our prayers would go with her. Then she started to cry, and none of us could think of anything to say. It was Patty who finally broke the silence, but all she said was, 'I'm going to miss my friends.' Peter took her back to the agency the next day, and we haven't seen her since.

"I'm embarrassed to admit it, but I felt a wonderful sense of exhilaration when Patty was finally gone. Still, it's amazing how often she comes to my mind. And whenever I think of her I stop what I'm doing and say a prayer for her. Even though she's no longer with us, in a strange way she remains a part of our family. I guess she always will. We did all we could do for her. It's just that the time came when we had no choice but to hand her over to the Lord. Her future is in His hands."

Perhaps because we were raised on fairy tales, we want every story to have a happy-ever-after ending, especially where children are concerned. Unfortunately in real life things don't always happen that way. They didn't for Henry and Claudia Greenley, and they didn't for Peter and Carol Ann Messina. They didn't for David, and they didn't for Patty.

MAKING A FINAL COMMITMENT

When you adopt a child, you make a commitment to do your very best to become a parent to him from the first moment that he moves into your home. You are not legally bound by this commitment, however, until the adoption becomes final. Once it is final, it's as if that child had been born to you. You are responsible for him in good times and in bad, in joy and in sorrow, in sickness and in health, until he is grown. There is no turning back.

If you have any doubts about being able to make a permanent life with the child, voice your concerns at once. Don't put it off until the adoption becomes final. In many cases you can delay the finalization until you are sure.

Meanwhile, seek help. Most adoption agencies have back-up resources that can offer counseling, advice and other types of assistance that they hope will help you to work out a solution. Even if your child was not adopted from a local agency, it will do its best to help. It wants the adoption to work.

Failed adoptions are unfortunate and sad for everyone involved. But sometimes a placement just doesn't work out. When this happens it's best to face the situation honestly. By continuing in an impossible relationship, you are creating a no-win situation. Remember that an adoption that was begun surrounded by prayer should end the same way.

If you are faced with the agonizing realities of a failed adoption you would do well to realize that there is such a thing as "successful failure." That is, what appears to be a dismal failure when viewed through man's eyes may actually be success when seen from God's point of view.

"I recently got a phone call from a friend of mine who is a school teacher in a nearby town," Carol Ann Messina reported. "Patty is in her eighth-grade class this year. She is also in her Sunday school class. Patty is now in another foster home and seems to be doing very well. Her foster parents are an older couple who treat her like a daughter. She is the only child in their home. That sounds like a perfect situation for Patty.

"My friend also told me that Patty talked to her about her faith in Jesus. Patty says that she accepted Him as her Savior while she was living with us. Her new foster parents aren't Christians, but Patty goes to church every Sunday. Once she told my friend, 'God is helping me to work out all my problems.' "

"We know without a doubt that God put Patty in our home," Peter added. "He put her here even though He knew from the beginning that she wouldn't be able to stay with us. Many, many times we have asked, 'Why did God set us up for such a failure?' I think I'm finally beginning to understand. This was God's way of bringing Patty to Himself. It really is true: God never, ever makes mistakes."

QUESTIONS FOR DISCUSSION

1. In your opinion, would David Greenley's adoption have worked out differently had Claudia and Henry handled it better? What could they have done?
2. When Carol Ann Messina learned that there was little hope of her ever being able to establish a loving mother-daughter relationship with Patty, how might she have made the best of the situation?
3. In determining their daughters' degree of freedom and privileges the Messinas compromised by sometimes overly restricting the responsible girls and at other times maintaining different sets of rules for the girls. What might have been a more successful approach to Patty's lack of responsibility?
4. What would you do in a situation like the Greenleys'? How about the Messinas'?

14. *The Children Speak*

Despite the many things that make them different and unique, there remains one constant principle in all adoptive families: the most important person in any adoption is the adopted child herself. Her feelings, her concerns, and her well-being must be the primary consideration of everyone involved. But because adults tend to limit their view of adoption to their own perspective, the questions and concerns of the children often go unanswered, their gentle wisdom and touching insights passing unnoticed. We do well to pause and listen as the children speak.

In this chapter you will read the thoughts and ideas about adoption from more than fifty children between the ages of seven and fifteen. A few adults who had grown up in adoptive homes also responded, as did some nonadoptive children who had particular thoughts on the subject based on their observations of classmates, friends, and relatives.

The positive feelings and attitudes toward adoption expressed by the majority of the children were impressive. One nine-year-old boy expressed it this way: "If people can't have a baby, then they should adopt one like my mom and dad did. There are lots of people who can't raise their own babies because it's too hard a job for them. I'm sure glad my parents wanted to adopt me. If no one wanted to, how could I ever have been in a family?"

"So what if I'm adopted?" asked a twelve-year-old girl. "My parents raised me and that's all I really care about. They love me and are very kind to me. They are my only real parents."

The idea of being special or chosen was a common theme, among the preadolescent children especially, perhaps because this is how their adoption was explained to them.

"I feel special to be adopted," said a seven-year-old girl. "Adopted isn't something everyone is."

"Adopted kids are chosen," stated a ten-year-old. "They are picked out because they are special."

Another ten-year-old said, "My parents aren't like most people who get their kids whether they want them or not. They wouldn't have gotten me if they didn't really want me."

"I'm not adopted," explained a boy in junior high school, "but I'm an only child because my mom can't have any more children. I've always wanted my parents to adopt another child so that I wouldn't be the only one. Lately they have been talking a lot about adopting a boy around seven or eight years old." Then he added, "I think that more people should adopt older children. Babies aren't the only ones who need homes."

"My stepdad is trying to adopt me," reported a twelve-year-old boy. "I sure hope it goes through, because he's already like a real dad to me. My other dad is trying to stop the adoption, but I don't know why. He never sees me or calls me on the phone or anything. I think he's just trying to punish me because I still love my mother and he doesn't."

Several adolescent children shared the view of a fourteen-year-old girl who said, "I wish I knew my birth parents. But if I did know them, it wouldn't change the way I feel about my adopted parents. I'll always love them most of all because they really wanted me and they took me when I needed a family."

"I think about my first mother a lot," a thirteen-year-old said thoughtfully. "I wish I had a picture of her. If I just knew what she looked like I'd be satisfied."

"I don't care about those other parents so much," said a fifteen-year-old boy, "but I wish I knew if I had any brothers or sisters. If I do, I would like to meet them. We might end up being really good friends."

Some responses, however, were not so positive. Interestingly, most of the negative comments came from adolescents. "I'm afraid my friends won't like me if they know I'm adopted," a twelve-year-old explained. "Like one time my best friend said, 'I sure would hate to be adopted, because then I wouldn't have any real parents'. I didn't say anything, because I didn't want her to find out I was adopted. I don't want anyone to know."

"I feel really mad at my real parents," declared a fourteen-year-old boy. "They cheated me out of the chance to be a normal kid who lives in a normal family. I don't want to be 'special' as everyone is always saying I am!"

An even stronger opinion was voiced by a thirteen-year-old girl. "I hate being adopted, and I think most other adopted kids do too," she said. "Sometimes I am kind of mean to my parents. I say bad things about them because I'm angry about being adopted. I have a brother and a sister who were born into our family and I feel like I'm different from them."

"Sometimes I feel I'm not wanted," said a fifteen-year-old boy. "I just don't feel that I really belong. My brothers are adopted, too, but they seem to fit in better than I do. Sometimes I feel as if I'm living with a bunch of strangers."

A surprising number of natural children either wish they were or believe that they are adopted. Some of them can be very hard to convince otherwise. This comment by an eleven-year-old girl was not uncommon: "My mother says that I'm not adopted, but I think I am. In lots of ways I seem like an adopted kid, and that's just how my parents treat me."

IMPRESSIONS AND FANTASIES

What exactly is an adopted child like? Not surprisingly, children's ideas are generally determined by the personalities of the adopted children they know. Here are some of the comments nonadoptive kids used to describe their adoptive counterparts:

"Adoptive kids are usually competitive."
"They're always loud."
"They're too quiet."
"Adopted kids act wild."
"Adopted kids hit or kick or bite when they get mad."
"They are poor students."
"They work hard."
"They never work."
"They're mean like Teresa who is adopted."
"They're nice and gentle."

It sounds as if the variations found among adopted kids are exactly the same as those found in any other group of children.

"My real parents might be nicer to me than my adopted parents are," suggested an eight-year-old boy. "They would probably get me more toys and stuff that I want."

But a fifteen-year-old girl observed, "I used to think that my birth parents would love me more than my adopted parents do. I guess all adopted kids think that. But now I know better. My birth parents probably wouldn't be nearly as nice to me, because they wouldn't want me as much."

"I think my first parents are probably movie stars," ventured an eight-year-old girl.

"Maybe my first father played football for the Dallas Cowboys," said a nine-year-old boy. "That's what I want to do."

"I used to dream that my birth parents were something special—famous or rich or important—but I grew out of that," recalled a fourteen-year-old boy. "Actually they probably weren't as good as my own parents are. They sure didn't love me as much."

Fantasizing about birth parents is common among adopted children, and it is very frustrating to many adoptive parents. How can any human being ever hope to compete with the rich, handsome, famous, perfect parents of a child's imagination? It seems that the best thing parents can do to help their child move from a world of fantasy to reality is to share with the children the truth concerning their biological pasts. Informed children are far less prone to fantasize than those who are kept in the dark.

"I was an unwanted baby born to a fifteen-year-old girl," related a thirty-four-year-old mother of two. "Fortunately for me, it wasn't so easy to get abortions in those days or I probably wouldn't be alive today. By means of adoption I became a part of a wonderful Christian family that was overjoyed to get me. It was God Himself who arranged for us to be together. The family in which I was raised was, is, and always will be my real family."

TO KNOW THE TRUTH

Today, almost without exception, professionals stress the importance of being honest with a child about his adoption. The kids agree. Without exception they said that they want to be told the truth, and they want to know it from the very beginning.

"My parents told me about my adoption when I was still really little," a ten-year-old girl said. "I'm glad they did. Can you believe that some parents don't even tell their children?"

"I got mad when I was told," said an eight-year-old boy, "because I was already in the first grade. My parents should have told me before that. I should have known when I was a baby."

Many share the opinion of a fifteen-year-old who said, "Parents should never, ever lie to their child about being adopted. If they would lie about something like that, how could their child ever believe anything else they say? Kids don't like parents who lie to them."

"Nobody had to tell me that I was adopted," a thirteen-year-old girl stated. "I can remember it. I was so glad to get a family who wanted to keep me forever. It's really hard for me to say 'I love you' to my parents, but I think they know how I feel." She paused. "At least I hope they do."

WANTING TO KNOW WHY

One of the most common concerns shared by adopted children is their struggle to find a satisfactory answer to the question, "Why was I given up by my birth parents?" The happiest children seem to be those who have come to terms with the explanation they were given by their adoptive parents. Many others, left to figure it out for themselves, assume that they were rejected because of some failure on their part.

"Obviously someone didn't want me," declared an eleven-year-old boy. "It makes me mad that that woman just dumped me without even telling anyone why."

"I always wondered why my birth mother gave me up," a fourteen-year-old pondered. "Was I ugly or no good or what?"

"I told my friends that I thought I was given up because I was ugly," related a thirteen-year-old girl, "and one of them said, 'Maybe so, but you are what you are.' That made me really feel bad. Another friend said, 'It's not what you look like that matters; it's what you are.' But my best friend, Kristin, told me, 'That couldn't be the reason. Mothers who give up their babies for adoption don't even see them first.' I hope Kristin is right."

Almost every child who does not know the facts attempts to guess his birth mother's reason for not keeping him. A large percentage of the children interviewed, especially the younger ones, agreed with the nine-year-old who reasoned, "Those first parents are probably dead. Adopted kids must be orphans." Many others shared this view of a thirteen-year-old girl: "My mother was probably too young and just couldn't handle a baby."

Where motive is concerned, most of the children were willing to give the biological mother the benefit of the doubt. They generally agreed that it had probably been very hard for her to give up her baby.

"She was probably too poor to keep me," a seven-year-old boy suggested. "She probably wanted me to be in a family that could afford to give me a nice home and warm clothes and good food and some nice toys."

"My first mother probably wanted me to have a better home than she could give me," reasoned an eleven-year-old girl.

A twelve-year-old said, "My parents told me that my birth mother must have loved me very much because she let me be adopted into a family that could give me a better life than she could."

"My mom told me that my birth mother agreed with her and my dad that children should grow up in families with two parents who really care for them and can give them a good home," said a fourteen-year-old girl. "They say that she couldn't give me that, so she arranged for me to be adopted by a family who could."

One twelve-year-old had a different idea. "I don't even try to guess why my first mother gave me up. I'm going to wait until I get older, then I will just find her and ask her."

REGARD FOR BIRTH MOTHERS

The kindness and sensitivity with which most children seem to regard their birth mothers is a credit to the gentle handling of a delicate situation by the adoptive parents.

166

"I'm sure my first mother didn't want to give me up," an eleven-year-old boy reflected. "It was probably a very hard thing for her to do. She did it for my own good, so that I could be raised in a family with parents who could take good care of me."

"She must have felt awful," observed a seven-year-old. "She must have cried and cried. I feel sorry for her."

A fifteen-year-old said, "She must have been terribly confused. I'm sure that she was sad and hurt. And frightened too. She must have been scared to death. That decision was probably very hard for her to make. You know, she was exactly the same age as I am right now. I can't imagine having to make a decision like that."

"I think she felt pressured to give me up," declared a twelve-year-old girl. "Then she probably felt guilty because she had done it."

A number of children commented on the feelings of guilt that they attribute to their biological mothers. A fourteen-year-old said, "That must have been the hardest decision she ever had to make. She must have felt as if she was torn into two pieces. She probably felt awfully guilty because she didn't know if she was doing the right thing or not. I never want to have to make a decision like that."

"I think adopted children should be grateful to the people who let them be adopted," said one ten-year-old. "Some mothers probably couldn't make the decision to give their babies up, so their kids had to grow up in a bad home."

"I really wish I knew if my mother had to give me up or if she just wanted to," said a twelve-year-old girl. "If she wanted to, I would be mad at her; but if she had to do it, I would feel sorry for her."

GROWING UP ADOPTED

Many adoptive parents feel that their adopted children have a harder time growing up, suffer more problems, and have more troublesome self-doubts than nonadoptive children. The opinions of adopted children are divided. One twelve-year-old said, "Adopted kids just have the same problems as everyone else," but another one declared, "All my problems are because

I'm adopted." A thirteen-year-old boy said, "The thing is, adopted kids just have one more thing to think about."

"My parents talk too much about my being adopted," commented an eight-year-old girl.

"My mother always says that I have more problems than other kids," stated a fifteen-year-old boy, "but in my opinion she's the one who causes the problems. She protects me too much. She wants to control my whole life. Why does she have to worry all the time? What's wrong with me that she can't just leave me alone?"

Evidently parents are not the only offenders. A nine-year-old boy told about his fourth-grade schoolteacher who, on the first day of school, had all the adopted children in the class stand up. There were three of them. "He told us that he had been adopted, too, so he could really understand us and our problems. The teacher said we would all be special friends that year. It was embarrassing."

A thirteen-year-old who was not an adopted child observed, "I think that some adopted kids make their own problems. They are always talking about their adoption. They keep on bragging about it like it's a great big deal or something."

Most of the adopted children agree. "I'm not ashamed of being adopted, but why talk about it all the time?" a twelve-year-old boy asked.

"My parents don't talk to other people about adopting my sister and me," said a nine-year-old. "If we want to tell people, we can, but they leave it up to us. We don't talk about it very much, but sometimes we do."

"I think about being adopted," said an eleven-year-old, "but I don't talk about it much because I think it bothers my parents. Sometimes I'd really like to talk to them about my adoption. I'd like to ask them some questions. But I don't, because I don't want to make them feel bad."

"Do you want to hear something funny?" laughed a ten-year-old girl. "Sometimes people who don't know that I'm adopted say I look just like my mother and sister. I don't tell them that I wasn't even born in the same family. I wonder what they would say if I did?"

TO TEASE OR NOT TO TEASE

Many parents express concern about the teasing their adopted children have to endure. Others, however, say that they are unaware of a problem. As for the adopted children themselves, only a few spoke of being teased by friends or schoolmates.

"The kids who get teased are the ones who are always talking about being adopted," observed an eleven-year-old girl.

"Everybody gets teased about something," a thirteen-year-old boy said. "If it's not about being adopted, then it's about having big ears or being dumb in math or something else."

"I've never heard anyone tease my adopted brother or my adopted friend, and I'm really glad," said a ten-year-old boy. "I'd get mad if anyone did."

But there were those who have encountered teasing, and they related some painful experiences. "I have a black friend who was adopted by a white family," said a fifteen-year-old boy. "People tease him by saying, 'Salt and pepper don't mix.' It's embarrassing to him."

"Sometimes people tease me by saying that I had to be adopted because I wasn't good enough for my real parents," said a nine-year-old.

A seven-year-old said, "One time my best friend got mad at me and said I was fat and stupid and adopted. So I got mad back and said she was ugly and dumb."

"Some boys in my class at school used to say that the reason I had to be adopted was because I was so ugly that when I was born my mother took one look at me and died of fright," said a twelve-year-old girl.

"My brother is the one who teases me," an eight-year-old girl commented. "When he gets mad he calls me a stupid adopted little kid. He's just as adopted as I am, but he never says anything about that!"

VULNERABLE BY ADOPTION

Yet, according to the kids, there are some areas in which adopted children seem to be especially vulnerable. "I think adopted kids suffer more psychologically, like feeling guilty and inferior and helpless," suggested a fifteen year-old-girl.

"Adopted kids can feel as if they aren't loved as much as other kids," said a nine-year-old.

A fourteen-year-old boy said, "Sometimes adopted kids don't get along too well with their parents." He paused, then added, "Of course, my brother has the same problem and he's not adopted."

"I think adopted kids sometimes stop obeying their parents because they feel that the adopted parents aren't their real parents and they wonder why they should have to obey them," said a thirteen-year-old.

Several children talked about having inner conflicts and questions, but many said that they did not discuss their concerns with anyone for fear of hurting their adoptive parents' feelings.

"I can't help worrying about why I wasn't wanted," said a nine-year-old girl. "Once I said something about it to my mom, but she said I shouldn't have such silly thoughts, then she changed the subject. I still worry about it, but now I don't tell my mom."

"My sister isn't adopted like me," observed an eight-year-old boy. "I always wonder which one of us my parents love the most."

"I just wish that I could know for positive sure that my parents love me and accept me just as much as they would if I had been born to them," explained a young teenager. "I really wish I knew, but how could I ever ask my parents something like that?"

A fourteen-year-old girl said, "Lots of times I wonder how my first mother looked and what she was like. But I'm afraid it would hurt my parents if I asked them, and I love them too much to do that."

"Sometimes at night I get to thinking about my natural parents, wondering who they are and why they gave me up, and I just can't get to sleep," commented a twelve-year-old girl. "I guess I would have to say that my biggest problem is insomnia."

An eleven-year-old girl questioned, "I wonder what my natural parents look like. I wonder if they're nice. Most of all I wonder if they ever think about me and wonder what I'm like."

WONDERING ... SEARCHING

Wondering about birth parents seems to be the greatest single common denominator among adopted children. Unfortunately the subject can be threatening to many adoptive parents.

"I just wish I knew what my birth mother looks like," said an eleven-year-old girl. "I wonder if she's good at drawing and bad in spelling like me. I wish I could see her and find out for myself."

A few children seem to be totally disinterested in their biological parents. "I never asked questions," said a twenty-five-year-old woman, "because there was nothing to ask. My mom and dad and sister are my family. What else do I need to know? I never had any desire to find my birth parents. I still don't."

"Everyone thinks that I should try to find my birth mother," said a fifteen-year-old girl, "but I don't want to. My parents have been very good to me, and I'm happy with things just the way they are. I don't want to change anything."

A fourteen-year-old reasoned, "If I ever did see my birth mother, what in the world would I say to her?"

When contemplating an actual search, many young people wisely consider the birth parents' viewpoint. Most feel that the birth parents would not be anxious to see their children again.

"I was adopted by parents who wanted me," explained a fifteen-year-old. "Why should I bother my birth parents? They didn't want me in the first place, and I'm sure that they wouldn't want to see me now."

"I think that my birth mother would be horrified if I suddenly came to see her," declared a fifteen-year-old. "She probably has a new family by now. How could she explain me to them?"

"I think my first mother would be mad at me for coming to see her," said a ten-year-old girl. "She would probably tell me to get away from her house and stay away."

"If I came to see her," suggested a thirteen-year-old, "it could ruin her whole life. It wouldn't be fair for me to do it."

"When she gave me up," observed a twelve-year-old boy, "she gave me up for good. It wouldn't be fair for me to show up and make her explain me to her husband and kids."

"That woman has a constitutional right to her privacy," declared a twenty-nine-year-old adoptee.

"I would be afraid to just knock on my birth mother's door," said a thirteen-year-old girl. "She probably wouldn't even let me in. Why should she? I'm a complete stranger."

"My mom told me that my biological mother is very intelligent," said a fifteen-year-old girl. "She gave me up so that she could finish school. I'd like to know what she did with her life, what kind of job she's in. But she probably wouldn't want to see me." She added, "I'm curious, but I'm not looking for a new mother. I like my present one just fine."

"I'm afraid that if I searched for my birth parents I would only end up hurting my adopted parents," said a twelve-year-old. "And I wouldn't hurt them for anything in the world!"

This concern was echoed by many adoptive children who feared that their real parents—the ones who had adopted and raised them—would feel hurt, unloved, dissatisfied, jealous, unwanted, left-out, or afraid of the competition. A few thought that such a search would be discouraged by their adoptive parents because the child could be hurt if he discovered something bad about his birth parents. Some thought that their adoptive parents might not mind such a search, and a few felt that their parents might encourage and help them.

"I knew that my mother was dead and that my father gave me up for adoption because he couldn't take care of me all alone," stated a fourteen-year-old girl. "I was really depressed and I used to cry a lot. My adopted parents thought it would be good for me to meet my father, so they helped me find him.

"I was scared when I found out where my real dad lived," the girl continued. "But when I called him, he was glad to talk to me. I met him, and we hugged and kissed. He said he would call me and he did. Now I visit him on a regular basis. I'm really glad I know him."

Whatever the reaction of the adoptive parents, for many children the desire to know persists. As one fifteen-year-old boy said, "All I want is to *see* my birth mother. I don't want to move in with her!"

"I've seen TV programs and I've read articles about kids who have searched out their birth parents," said a fourteen-year-old girl. "Those stories always seemed to have happy-ever-after endings. But I really don't think it happens that way very often."

It doesn't. Few experiences end happily. Most ultimately fall somewhere between disappointing and disastrous.

"I asked my parents' lawyer about finding my birth parents, and he said it was very hard because of the sealed records," said a fifteen-year-old. "He said most searches are unsuccessful."

"Most searchers probably just get tired and give up," suggested a fourteen-year-old. "Maybe they really don't want to find their birth parents as much as they think they do."

"If I ever found my other parents," said a twelve-year-old, "I would probably end up getting the door slammed in my face. I'm sure there would be a sad ending for me."

"Most adopted kids would probably be very disappointed if they did find their birth parents," observed a thirteen-year-old boy. "The parents probably wouldn't be at all what the kid thought they would be."

"My mom showed me an article she read about a man who searched out his birth mother," stated a thirteen-year-old. "The whole thing turned out badly for everyone. In the end he said he wished he had never started his search. I never will."

"I have the very best kind of parents right now," explained a fourteen-year-old boy. "They listen to me when I want to talk, they answer me when I ask them questions, and they leave me alone when I want to be left alone. They love me just as I am because I'm their son. Why would I ever want to look for any other parents?"

QUESTIONS FOR DISCUSSION

1. From what the children expressed, do you think it is important that an adoptee be given all the information available on his background? In what ways can that information help him? In what ways may it be of harm?

2. Is it possible for adoptive parents to create a situation free and open enough to allow their children to be able to express these thoughts to their parents? If not, why not? If so, how might this be accomplished?

15.   *Conclusion*

Now you have today's adoption story. You have heard the good news and the bad news. There have been words of encouragement and words of discouragement. It is important to see both sides. To accept the positive and refuse to see the negative is unrealistic and can only lead to disappointment.

If this were a movie, you could take your newly adopted child into your arms and as a family happily fade into the sunset. But real life is not like that. Your family experiences will sometimes be pleasant, at other times unpleasant. Your family will go through these experiences, good or bad, together. Sometimes you and your child will enjoy each other. At other times you will grow impatient. It is the experiences you share day by day—the smiles, the laughter, the sighs, and the tears—that bind you together into a real family.

What, then, are the most important things to remember about the current adoption scene? They can be summed up in eight points.

- *In any adoption the welfare of the child must be the first and foremost consideration of everyone involved.* It may well be that receiving your child, holding him in your arms, and sharing the joy of his entry into your family is the happiest moment of your life. I hope that is so. Nevertheless, an adoption is no longer considered to be merely a means of finding a baby for a specific family. It is finding the right home for a specific child. Understanding this will help you to be more patient with the questions, the screening, the home study, and the waiting you may be asked to endure.
- *There definitely are children available.* It may not be the two-day-old girl with blond curls that you had pictured in your dreams, but there are plenty of children. Give some consideration to the minority children, those with

handicaps, and the older children who are available and waiting for homes. You may discover that one of these children is just perfect for you. It has happened that way in many families.

- *Not everyone should adopt.* It is vitally important to examine your motives honestly and determine why you want to adopt. Be sure your reasons are valid ones. Then take a long, realistic look at your present family situation. Be sure that a child would fit in and be a welcome part of your family. Remember that when the newness wears off, the child will still be there, and he will still be yours.

- *Maintain a family where love, openness, honesty, and a strong faith in God are a natural way of life.* Many of the problems that exist between adoptive parents and their children, just as in nonadoptive families, can be traced to a lack of communication, open sharing, and understanding.

- *Anticipate problems.* It is not being overpessimistic to expect that problems will occur. Happy-ever-after endings belong in fairy tales, not in real life. If you anticipate problems, you will be better equipped to handle them when they hit. And you will be less likely to react in word or action in ways that you will regret later. If the problems never materialize, so much the better.

- *There are no guarantees.* Like biological children, your adopted children may or may not turn out the way you want them to. Parenthood holds no guarantees. Nor does life. Love means accepting another person for who and what he is and not demanding that he change to fit into all your dreams and expectations. We have an awesome responsibility to "train up a child in the way he should go." But once we have trained our children, we must be willing and prepared to let them go to make their own decisions and lead their own lives. We cannot and should not accept responsibility for the life they choose to build for themselves.

- *God has the answers.* When problems come that seem too painful to bear, and when your questions seem unanswerable, you must trust God to work it all out. That is more easily said than done. But easy or hard, it is the truth. To deny it is to deny either God's total love for you or His sovereign power over your life. God is not bound by the limits of understanding and short-sightedness as we are. He sees the finished picture, and He promised that it will be beautiful. Trust Him to be true to His promises. Let Him prove His faithfulness.

- *A grafted family tree can be every bit as strong, beautiful, and fruitful as any other family tree.* Don't let anyone tell you otherwise. You will hear good adoption stories and bad ones. You will hear happy accounts that will warm your very soul, and you will hear sad ones that will wrench your heart. Listen to them all, but do not lose your perspective. Determine that your family's story will be one of the good ones.

The fact that your adopted child was not born to you should not make the least bit of difference in your day-to-day living. You will care for her, teach her, encourage her, love her, and discipline her exactly as you would if she were yours by birth. If you allow the fact that she is adopted to color your daily dealings with her, you will be putting an unnecessary strain on your relationship.

Do your best for your child. Help her to develop what she has within her so that she will be able to cope with her own future. No parent can do any more.

We have looked at some of the special needs and problems your adopted child may have. Some are related to her adoption, but most are not. That she is adopted is a fact of your child's existence. She and you must learn to accept this fact. You cannot change it, and you shouldn't try. But neither should you exaggerate the importance of this fact. There is nothing to be gained by overemphasizing a child's adoption and making him feel different.

Whatever your adoption experience, it is unique. That's because you are unique, and so is your child. You will not feel exactly the same as any other adoptive parent, nor will you act exactly the same. But there are some things that you will have in common. All adoptive parents want to raise their children to become responsible, contributing members of society. They all want to share a happy family life with them.

Children are a gift from God. They are also our greatest

and most precious natural resource. Through adoption a child becomes a cherished member of your family. And while she is doing so, she will surely make your life richer and fuller.

OPEN FORUM

KAREN ALVARADO: *Our little girl had her third birthday last week. We had a big day—a party with her little friends in the afternoon and then a big family dinner in the evening. She fell asleep on my lap. As I tucked her into bed I prayed, "Bless the girl who gave birth to Jodie. Please let her know that this little girl is safe, happy, and very dearly loved. Give that girl happiness, too, and somehow bring her to yourself."*

JUDY RANDLE: *When you see them so peaceful and happy, it's easy to forget the hard times and the frustrations and struggles, isn't it? All you can think of is how deeply and richly God has blessed your family.*

ROGER CRAWFORD: *Whether we give birth to our children or adopt them, we don't own them. They're only on loan to us from the Lord God. It's our job to raise them, to teach them and love them wisely, to parent them the very best we know how, and to root and ground them in the Lord. If we do these things, we will have accomplished the job that He has called us to do. Then we must be willing to commit them to God for safekeeping. Our children will be better people because of us, and our lives will be better and more complete because of them.*

APPENDIX 1

STATE POLICIES ON ADOPTIONS

The following table summarizes adoption laws state by state and gives the names and addresses of state agencies that can provide a listing of adoption agencies within a state. This comparison chart is intended only as a general guide. Laws and policies regarding adoption can be changed in any state at any time. You should refer specific questions to a licensed adoption agency in your area or to an attorney who is familiar with your state's current adoption laws and policies.

State	Independent Adoptions Permitted?	Subsidies Offered?	Judicial Termination of Parental Rights Required?	Birth Records Opened Without Court Order?	State Agencies
Alabama	Yes	Sometimes	No	Allows adult adoptees the original birth certificate	Bureau of Child Welfare Administrative Bldg. 64 No. Union St. Montgomery, AL 36104
Alaska	Yes	No	Yes	No	Dept. of Health and Social Services Pouch H-05 Juneau, AK 99811
Arizona	Yes	Medical	No	No	Dept. of Economic Security P.O. Box 6123 Phoenix, AZ 85005
Arkansas	Yes	For children with special problems	No	No	Arkansas Social Services P.O. Box 1437 Little Rock, AR 72203
California	Yes	Yes	In some cases	No	Adoption Services Section Social Services Div. 714 P Street Sacramento, CA 95814
Colorado	Yes	In a few cases	Yes	No	Div. of Title XX Services Dept. of Social Services 1575 Sherman Street Denver, CO 80203

State					Address
Connecticut	Yes, if placed by parent or relative	Yes, for hard-to-place children	Yes	No	Dept. of Children and Youth Services 345 Main St. Hartford, CT 06115
Delaware	No, unless adopted by step-parent or blood relative	In a few cases	Yes	No	Dept. of Health and Social Services Div. of Social Services Box 309 Wilmington, DE 19899
District of Columbia	No, unless adopted by step-parent or blood relative	Yes	In some cases	No	Bureau of Family Services Social Rehabilitation Administration 122 C St., NW Washington, DC 20001
Florida	Yes	No	Yes	No	Office of Social and Economic Services P.O. Box 2050 Jackson, FL 32203
Georgia	Yes	In a few cases	No	No	Div. of Social Services Dept. of Human Resources 47 Trinity, SW Room 211-8 Atlanta, GA 30334
Hawaii	Yes	Yes	Yes	No	Dept. of Social Services P.O. Box 339 Honolulu, HI 96809

State	Independent Adoptions Permitted?	Subsidies Offered?	Judicial Termination of Parental Rights Required?	Birth Records Opened Without Court Order?	State Agencies
Idaho	Yes	Medical	Yes	No	Dept. of Health and Welfare Statehouse Boise, ID 83702
Illinois	Yes	Yes	Yes	No	Dept. of Children and Family Services 632 E. Adams St. Springfield, IL 62706
Indiana	Yes, but official approval needed unless by step-parent or relative.	Yes, for hard-to-place children	No	No	Social Services Div. State Dept. of Public Welfare 1415 Meridian St. Indianapolis, IN 46225
Iowa	No	Medical	No	No	Bureau of Family and Adult Services Div. of Community Services Lucas State Office Bldg. Des Moines, IA 50319
Kansas	Yes	Medical	Yes	Allows adult adoptee or guardian of minor access to original birth certificate	Child Welfare Services State Dept. of Social Welfare State Office Bldg. Topeka, KS 66612

State					
Kentucky	Yes, with approval of Commission of Child Welfare	Yes	No	No	Dept. of Child Welfare 403 Wapping St. Frankfort, KY 40601
Louisiana	Yes	No	No	No	Child Welfare Dept. of Public Welfare P.O. Box 44065 Baton Rouge, LA 70804
Maine	Yes, with study by a licensed agency	Yes	Sometimes	State maintains voluntary contact files for adoptees and birth parents	Dept. of Human Services State House Augusta, ME 04330
Maryland	Yes, if placed by parent or relative	Yes, for hard-to-place children	Yes	No	Dept. of Human Resources Social Services Admin. 1315 Saint Paul Baltimore, MD 21202
Massachusetts	No, unless adopted by step-parent or blood relative	Medical	—	No	Div. of Family and Children's Services Office of Social Services 600 Washington St. Boston, MA 02111
Michigan	Yes, if placed by parent, relative, or guardian	Medical	Yes	No	State Dept. of Social Services 300 South Capitol Lansing, MI 48926

State	Independent Adoptions Permitted?	Subsidies Offered?	Judicial Termination of Parental Rights Required?	Birth Records Opened Without Court Order?	State Agencies
Minnesota	No, but restriction may be waived by court	Medical	Yes	Adoptees over 21 have limited access to birth certificate	Dept. of Public Welfare Centennial Bldg. St. Paul, MN 55755
Mississippi	Yes	Not specified	No, but court accepts voluntary consent	No	State Dept. of Public Welfare Box 4321 Fondren Station Jackson, MS 39216
Missouri	Yes	Medical	In some cases	No	Division of Welfare Family Services Broadway St. Office Bldg. Jefferson City, MO 65101
Montana	Yes	For children with handicaps	Yes	No	Social Services Bureau State Dept. of Public Welfare Helena, MT 59601
Nebraska	Yes, if placed by parent	Medical	No	Allows adoptee at age 25 access to name of relatives or to original birth certificate if consent form has been filed by relatives.	Dept. of Public Welfare 1526 K St., 4th Floor Lincoln, NE 68508

State					Address
Nevada	No	Medical	No	No	Welfare Div. Dept. of Human Resources 251 Jeanell Dr. Capitol Mall Complex Carson City, NV 89701
New Hampshire	Yes	No, with rare exceptions	Yes	No	Bureau of Child and Family Services State Dept. of Health and Welfare 8 Loudon Rd. Concord, NH 03301
New Jersey	Yes, if placed by parent	In some cases	Yes	State registry for adult adoptees and birth parents	Div. of Youth and Family Services Dept. of Institutions and Agencies Box 510 Trenton, NJ 08625
New Mexico	No, but exceptions made for relatives and stepparents	Sometimes	No	No	Field Mgr., Adoption Services P.O. Box 2348 Santa Fe, NM 87501
New York	Yes, if placed by parent, relative, or guardian	In some cases	No	No	N.Y. State Dept. of Social Services 1450 Western Ave. Albany, NY 12203

State	Independent Adoptions Permitted?	Subsidies Offered?	Judicial Termination of Parental Rights Required?	Birth Records Opened Without Court Order?	State Agencies
North Carolina	Yes	No, with some rare exceptions	No	No	Children's Services Branch Div. of Social Services Dept. of Human Resources 325 N. Salisbury St. Raleigh, NC 27611
North Dakota	Yes	Medical	No	No	Community Services Social Services Board Capitol Bldg. Bismark, ND 58505
Ohio	Yes, under certain conditions	In some cases	Yes	No	Dept. of Rehabilitation and Welfare 30 E. Broad St. Columbus, OH 43215
Oklahoma	Yes	Only prior to finalization	No	No	Div. of Services to Youth and Children Social and Rehabilitative Services State Dept. of Institutions P.O. Box 25352 Oklahoma City, OK 73125
Oregon	Yes, if placed by relatives	In some cases	——	No	Adoption Dept. Children's Services Div. Dept of Human Resources 509 Public Service Bldg. Salem, OR 97310

State					Address
Pennsylvania	Yes	Yes, for hard-to-place children	Yes	No	State Dept. of Public Welfare Bureau of Child Welfare Health and Welfare Bldg. P.O. Box 2675 Harrisburg, PA 17120
Rhode Island	Yes, if placed by relative	Yes	Yes	No	Child Welfare Service Div. of Community Services 600 New London Ave. Cranston, RI 02920
South Carolina	Yes	Not specified	No	No	Dept. of Social Services P.O. Box 1520 Columbia, SC 29202
South Dakota	Yes	Yes	Yes	No	State Dept. of Public Welfare Service Administrator Pierre, SD 57501
Tennessee	Yes, if placed by parents	Yes	Yes	No	Social Services Dept. of Human Services State Office Bldg. / Rm. 310 Nashville, TN 37219
Texas	Yes	In some cases	Yes	No	Div. of Special Services Dept. of Public Welfare John H. Regan Bldg. Austin, TX 78701

State	Independent Adoptions Permitted?	Subsidies Offered?	Judicial Termination of Parental Rights Required?	Birth Records Opened Without Court Order?	State Agencies
Utah	Yes	Medical	Yes	No	Utah Div. of Family Services 333 So. Second East Salt Lake City, UT 84111
Vermont	Yes	In some cases	Yes	No	Div. of Social Services Dept. of Social and Rehabilitation Services 81 River St. Montpelier, VT 05602
Virginia	In limited cases	Medical	In some cases	No	Div. of Social Services Dept. of Welfare P.O. Box K-176 Richmond, VA 23288
Washington	Yes, with permission of court	—	Yes	No	Dept. of Social and Health Services P.O. Box 1788 Olympia, WA 98504
West Virginia	Yes	No	No	No	Department of Welfare Div. of Social Services 1900 Washington St., East Charleston, WV 25305

Wisconsin	No; court assigns agency to give report	Medical	Yes	No	Dept. of Health and Social Services Div. of Family Services State Office Bldg. / Rm. 300 1 West Wilson St. Madison, WI 53702
Wyoming	Yes	No	Yes	No	Dept. of Health and Social Services Div. of Public Assistance and Social Services Hathaway Bldg. Cheyenne, WY 82001

APPENDIX 2

RESOURCES FOR ADOPTIVE PARENTS

The following list is a resource for people who are considering adoption or who would like to have contact with a parent support group. Because the United States has a mobile and changing society, there may be changes in address, membership, purposes, or programs offered. When you write for information, be sure to enclose a self-addressed stamped envelope.

ADOPTIVE PARENTS COMMITTEE, INC.
210 Fifth Avenue
New York, NY 10010
This organization has the facts on U.S. adoption agencies including fees, the availability of children, etc. It can also help with sources of foreign children and with independent adoptions.

AID TO THE ADOPTION OF SPECIAL CHILDREN (AASK)
Box 11212
Oakland, CA 94611
This nonprofit foundation was established to help older, minority, and handicapped children find permanent homes. It can give you information and provides supportive services such as financial aid, counseling, and legal material. AASK has a number of local chapters.

BETHANY CHRISTIAN SERVICES
901 Eastern Avenue, NE
Grand Rapids, MI 49503
Adoption services is only one of the many kinds of family services offered by this organization. Bethany has a number of branch offices across the country.

CHRISTIAN ADOPTION AND FAMILY SERVICES
17150 Norwalk Blvd., Suite 117
Cerritos, CA 90701
This organization provides adoption and counseling programs. At present placements are made only in Southern California.

190

COUNCIL OF ADOPTIVE PARENTS (CAP)
67 Wood Haven Drive
Rochester, NY 14625
This organization is involved in many different aspects of adoption including conferences on the older child and on racial identity.

EVANGELICAL CHILD AND FAMILY AGENCY
1530 North Main Street
Wheaton, IL 60187
This agency places both babies and hard-to-place children in evangelical Christian homes. They also have a foster-care program. Placements are made only within a fifty-mile or so radius of Chicago.

HOLT ADOPTION PROGRAM
P.O. Box 2880
Eugene, OR 97402
This organization is mostly concerned with the adoption of children from Asian countries.

INTERNATIONAL CONCERNS COMMITTEE FOR CHILDREN
911 Cypress Drive
Boulder, CO 80303
This organization is especially concerned with foreign and special-needs children. It provides counseling and agency information. There are branches in Newton, Maine, and in Allentown, Pennsylvania.

NORTH AMERICAN COUNCIL ON ADOPTABLE CHILDREN
1340 Connecticut Avenue, NW / Suite 229
Washington, DC 20036
This organization concentrates on special-needs children. It can provide the names of parent groups in your area and can put you in touch with local adoption agencies.

ORGANIZATION OF FOSTER FAMILIES FOR EQUALITY AND REFORM (OFFER)
239 Vincent Drive
East Meadow, NY 11554
This organization is concerned with all aspects of foster care and is working to support legislation and policy that will keep foster care from becoming a dead end for children.

CHOSEN FAMILIES

ORGANIZATION FOR A UNITED RESPONSE (OURS)
3307 Highway 100 N., Suite 203
Minneapolis, MN 55422
This is a national support group that reports which agencies are taking applications for foreign and U.S. adoptions, what kinds of children are available, and the costs and requirements. It can also provide a list of parent support groups.

PARENTS FOR LOVING ADOPTIONS NOW (PLAN)
P.O. Box 667
McMinnville, OR 97128
PLAN is involved with multiracial and international adoptions and the needs of special children. It accepts adoption applications.

PERMANENT FAMILIES FOR CHILDREN
Child Welfare League of America, Inc.
67 Irving Place
New York, NY 10003
This organization can provide the names of adoption agencies in your area. It publishes *Waiting Children,* which features the pictures and biographies of special-needs children.

SOUTH AMERICAN MISSIONARY EVANGELISM (S.A.M.E.)
P.O. Box 2344
Bismark, ND 58502
This organization provides domestic and foreign adoption services, though it focuses on placing abandoned children of Brazil and Colombia.

APPENDIX 3

SUGGESTED READING

These books will offer extra information on several aspects of the adoptive experience. Books written from a Christian perspective are so noted.

Dobson, James C. *Hide and Seek*. Old Tappan, N.J.: Fleming H. Revell, 1974.
Not specifically concerned with adoption, but written from a Christian perspective with a very good section on self-esteem of children.

Feingold, Ben F. *Why Your Child Is Hyperactive*. New York: Random House, 1974.
An informative book on the whole area of hyperactivity in children, written by a medical doctor.

Martin, Cynthia D. *Beating the Adoption Game*. San Diego: Oak Tree Publications, 1980.
Discussion of all aspects of adoption, pointing out some of the abuses and red tape encountered by people wishing to adopt.

Phillips, Carolyn. *Our Family Got a Stepparent*. Ventura, Calif.: Regal Books, 1979.
A book for children explaining the problems and feelings that can be expected when a new parent is introduced into the family.

Wender, Paul H., and Estelle Wender. *The Hyperactive Child*. New York: Crown, 1978.
An excellent book on the problem of hyperactivity written by two experts in the field.

Wheeler, Bonnie. *Challenged Parenting*. Ventura, Calif.: Regal Books, 1982.
Explained by subtitle: *A Practical Handbook for Parents of Children With Handicaps*. Written from Christian perspective.

Wishard, Laurie, and William Wishard. *Adoption, the Grafted Tree*. New York: Avon Books, 1979.
Practical, psychological, and legal information about all aspects of the adoption process.

INDEX

Who Am I?

Who Are My Parents?

KAY MARSHALL STROM

CONTENTS

1. *Who Am I?*

My name is Rebecca and I am twelve years old. I live in a white, two-story house with my mom and dad and my big brother Mark. We have twenty-one pets—two dogs, two cats, and seventeen goldfish.

Mark is a pretty nice brother most of the time. We play checkers and Monopoly together. He is teaching me how to throw a football the right way. He helps me with my homework when everyone else is too busy. But sometimes Mark teases me, and sometimes he gets grouchy. When he gets angry, he calls me names. Then I don't like him so much.

Mom says that Mark and I are just like any other brother and sister. I guess that is true in most ways, but in one way we are different. Mark and I are adopted.

Ever since I can remember I have known about being adopted. Here is how it happened in our family. When Mom and Dad got married, they wanted to have children. They waited and they waited. For seven years they waited, but no baby was born to them. But Mom and Dad didn't give up. They knew that there were people who had children they could not take care of, so my parents decided they would adopt some of those kids.

My brother Mark was first. Because he was two years old when he came into the family, he can't remember anything about it. Mom and Dad liked Mark so much that they decided they wanted another child. So they applied one more time at the adoption agency. Then they started waiting again. They waited for two years. At last they got the phone call they had been waiting for. The agency had a baby ready for them—a baby girl. That baby was me!

When Mom and Dad brought me home, Grandpa was

waiting in the driveway with his movie camera. He took pictures of me sleeping in the car, of Mom trying to feed me while I was sleeping, of everyone holding me while I was sleeping. I sure was a lazy kid!

I love to look at those pictures. Mark was very funny. He kept petting my head as if I were a little kitten. You would never believe how tiny I was!

One time I asked Mom if she and Dad were disappointed that they had to adopt babies instead of having some born to them. She seemed surprised that I asked. She said, "Disappointed? We are glad! Why, if we had been able to have babies, we would never have gotten you and Mark."

In a lot of ways Mom and Dad and Mark and I are alike, but we are all different, too. My hair is darker than anyone else's, and it is curly. Mom is the only one with blue eyes, and Mark is the only one with freckles. I am pretty good in music—I can play the piano and the flute. My brother is awful in music, but he is a really good football player.

Mom and Dad say that they are not musical or athletic. But they want Mark and me to grow in our own ways and to develop the talents God gave us. That is why they encourage us so much. They bought me a piano so that I can take lessons. They never miss any of Mark's games. Mom says our birth parents must have been very talented to have made children like us.

Most of the time I don't even think about being adopted. Sometimes, though, things happen that put questions in my mind. Then I feel bothered till I get some answers.

One thing that made me start wondering was a school project that our class is doing. We have been tracing our roots, finding out all about our great-grandparents and what countries our ancestors came from and all that. I don't know any of that stuff about me. I don't even know about the woman I was born to.

I talked to my family about the project. My mom said she didn't know very much about my birth parents either, except that the woman was part Spanish. I guess that is where I got my dark hair.

Then my dad said, "When you were adopted into our family, you became a part of us. Our ancestors are your ancestors."

"Yeah," Mark said. "Just like Mom and Dad's parents are our grandparents."

That makes a lot of sense to me. I know my Grandma and Grandpa really well. They live only two miles away from us. And no one could ever love me more than they do. They have time for me when everyone else is too busy to be bothered. They tell me stories about when they were young, and they like it when I ask them questions.

One day I asked my grandpa if he thought Mom and Dad could really understand what it felt like to be adopted. You know what he said? He said, "Rebecca, every one of us in this family is adopted—you and Mark, your mom and dad, Grandma and me—all of us."

I could hardly believe it! Dad looks just like the pictures in our family album of Grandpa when he was younger. Could it be true that my dad was adopted?

Grandpa must have seen the surprised look on my face, because he started to laugh. He said, "I guess I should explain what I mean. We were not all adopted by the parents who raised us. We were all adopted by God. Remember when you asked Jesus into your heart? That's when you were adopted into God's family. Since each one of us has done that, all of us are God's adopted children."

So adoption was all God's idea in the first place. We made our family the same way He made His. I like that.

Another time when I was wondering about things, Grandma told Mark and me some stories from the Bible about children who were a little bit like us. They were not raised by the people they were born to, either. One of them was Samuel. From the time he was a little boy he lived in the temple with Eli the priest. Eli took care of him and taught him about God.

Joseph was another one. He was kidnapped by his own brothers and taken away to Egypt to live as a slave. Can you imagine that? My brother would never treat me like that! Not even when he's angry with me. But in the end it all worked out well for Joseph and his family, because Joseph was able to save them all from starving to death during a famine.

Mark's favorite story is the one about Moses. Moses' own family loved him a lot, and they wanted to keep him with them. But they could not because of the cruel Egyptian king. After he was adopted by the king's own daughter, however, Moses was raised to be a prince in the royal palace of Egypt. Many years later he was able to get all his people out of that country.

Esther is my favorite. She was the Jewish girl who became queen of Persia. Even though it meant risking her own life, she went before the king and begged him to spare the lives of her people, the Jews, which he did. If it had not been for Esther, they all would have been killed.

All these stories really happened. You can find them in the Bible and read them for yourself if you want to. The exciting thing about these Bible people is that God put each one of them in just the right place for a special reason. One time I asked Mark if he thought that God had put us with our mom and dad for a very special reason, too. He just shrugged his shoulders and said, "Who knows?" I guess he doesn't think about things like that as much as I do.

But I could not stop wondering about it. I asked my parents what they thought. Dad said, "God does everything for a special reason, Rebecca. He put you in our family because that's exactly where He wants you."

"But why?" I asked.

"Because this is where you belong," he said. "Because God made you to be our daughter."

2. *Who Are My Real Parents?*

I know a little girl named Jenny who lives two houses away from me. She just started kindergarten. My friend Linda and I walk with her to school every morning.

Jenny is adopted too, but she doesn't look anything like her parents. Her mother has blond, curly hair; her father has red hair. Both of them have blue eyes. But Jenny's hair is straight and black, and her dark brown eyes are almond-shaped. That's because Jenny is half Korean. Her parents adopted her from an orphanage in Korea.

One day after Linda and I dropped Jenny off at the kindergarten room at school, Linda said, "Poor Jenny! I would hate to be adopted like her. Just think, she will never know who her parents are."

I said, "That's silly, Linda! She lives with her parents."

"That is not what I mean," Linda said. "I mean that she will never know her *real* parents. You know, the ones she was born to."

I knew *exactly* what Linda meant, and I decided it would be best to drop the subject right there. I have heard all that stuff about "real parents" before. Kids are always asking me, "Don't you even know your *real* parents?" And I will admit that I have done a lot of thinking and wondering about that myself.

It used to be that whenever I talked about the people I was born to, I would call them my "real parents." I would say things like "I wonder what my real mother looked like?" or "Were my real parents German or English or Italian or what?"

My mom and dad always tried to answer my questions the best they could. But my dad would always end up by saying, "Rebecca, *we* are your real parents. We took you as our daughter when you were just a tiny baby. After you were with us for almost a year, we were finally able to go to court and sign the papers that made your adoption final. We will never forget that day, because that was when the judge finally declared you legally our child. That is how you came into our family. But to us it is no different than if you had been born to Mom and me."

I know that whole story. I have heard it lots of times. But sometimes I wonder, is it *really* the same as if I had been born to them? There are times when my parents do things that seem very unfair to me. They make me eat broccoli and spinach and other foods I hate when it would be just as easy to cook things I like, such as pizza or spaghetti. I have to go to bed when I am not the least bit tired. I have to do homework and practice the piano when all of my friends are playing and watching television. And that's another thing—I don't get to watch nearly as much television as other kids do. The thing is, my friends' parents let them do a lot of things that my mom and dad won't let me do.

Last year I loved horses more than anything else in the whole world. One night before dinner I asked my dad very nicely if he would please get me a horse of my own. He said no. I tried to explain how important it was to me and that I would take care of the horse and would even help find a place to keep it. But my dad just said, "Now, Rebecca, we have been through all this before. We cannot afford a horse." Then he went right back to reading his newspaper. He wouldn't even talk about it with me.

All of a sudden I got really mad and I yelled, "I wish I lived with my *real* parents! I'll bet that they would get me a horse! They'd care about the things that are really important to me!"

"You sure are dumb, Rebecca!" my brother Mark said. "You are living with your real parents right now. What do you think Mom and Dad are?" I could tell from his voice and the way he was looking at me that he was pretty disgusted.

Mom and Dad didn't say anything. I could not think of anything to say, either, which is pretty unusual for me. So we all just stood there and looked at each other. I was feeling pretty bad about yelling at my dad like that. I was also embarrassed and confused. Finally I ran to my room, where I could be alone. I needed time to think things over.

Just what are *real* parents anyway? Are they the ones who make a child, or are they the ones who raise him? If someone's parents look really different from them like Jenny's parents do, can they still be real parents?

While I was wondering about all this, I suddenly remembered something I had read in *The Velveteen Rabbit,* about what it means to be real. I went to my bookcase, found the book, and looked up that part so that I could read it again.

The Velveteen Rabbit is about a little toy stuffed rabbit whose greatest wish is to be real. The problem is, he doesn't really understand what being real means. So the rabbit asks the wise old toy horse who lives in the playroom with him just what "real" is. This is what the horse said:

> "Real isn't how you are made. It's a thing that happens to you. When a child loves you for a long, long time, not just to play with, but REALLY loves you, then you become real.
> *"It doesn't happen all at once. You become. It takes a long time. That's why it doesn't often happen to people who break easily, or have sharp edges, or who have to be carefully kept."**

I think that horse really knew what he was talking about, don't you? What he said is just as true for parents as it is for toys. Parents who are not able to keep their children are the kind of people who break easily. It takes a lot of time and a lot of work to become real parents. It takes a lot of love, too. And do you know what? That sounds a lot like my own mom and dad.

Mom and Dad are the ones who did all of the no-fun stuff for me like changing my diapers and feeding me in the middle of the night and taking care of me when I was sick. They are the ones who have always helped and encouraged me. They are the

---

*Margery Williams, *The Velveteen Rabbit* (New York: Avon, 1975), 17. Used by permission.

ones who took me to Sunday school and church and helped me to understand about being God's child.

Mom and Dad are the ones who put up with me when I am grumpy and comfort me when I am sad. They listen to me when I need to talk. They answer me when I ask them questions. They leave me alone when I need to be left alone. They are always there when I need them. They love me just because I am me. Doesn't that sound like real parents to you? It does to me.

It was silly for me to think that my birth parents could love me more than my mom and dad do. When I really think about it, I know that they never could.

I am glad that those first parents gave me life. Without them I would not even be alive. But they are not my real parents. My real parents are my mom and dad, the ones who love me and care for me every day. No matter whatever happens or how old I get, they will always be my real parents.

I wonder if Jenny is too young to understand about real parents? Someday I will tell her.

3.   *Why Was I Given Up?*

My mom and dad don't often talk about Mark's and my adoption with people outside our family. They say it is up to us to decide who we want to tell and when. Mark doesn't tell anyone. He says that it is nobody else's business. Although I don't see any reason to talk about it all the time like some kids do, I really don't care if people know.

One night when my friend Linda was sleeping over at my house, she told me that she was born in Germany. Her dad was in the army over there. Then she asked me where I was born. I said I didn't know because I was adopted. At first she didn't believe me.

"You look too much like the rest of your family to be adopted," she said.

I said, "Maybe so, but I was adopted just the same."

Then Linda asked, "How come the woman you were born to didn't keep you herself?"

I said I didn't know, which is the truth.

Actually, I've wondered that same thing myself lots of times. It is quite obvious that my birth mother didn't want me, or else she would not have given me up. But it seems as if she would have to have had a pretty good reason for not wanting me, and I surely do wish I knew what her reason was.

All the next day I thought about Linda's question. I could not get it out of my mind. When I came home from school, my mom was in the kitchen making brownies. I poured myself a glass of milk, sat down at the table, and asked, "Mom, do you know why I was given up for adoption?"

She said she did not know why.

"Maybe my birth mother was really poor," I suggested.

"Maybe she could not afford to buy food and clothes and toys for me."

"That's possible," Mom said. "Still, there are many, many poor families who manage to do a very good job of raising their children. No matter how hard times get, Dad and I would never consider giving up you or your brother. We would all stick together, share whatever we had, and get by the best way we could."

"She may be dead," I suggested. "She could have died when I was born."

Mom shook her head. "No," she said. "I am sure that's not it. She is the one who signed the adoption papers, remember."

I waited a long time before I told Mom my other idea. I didn't even like to think about it myself. But finally I came right out and said it. "Maybe I wasn't cute enough for her." Even though it sounded terrible, I had to admit that it was a good possibility. If you could see me, you would know what I mean. I am not at all pretty. I am really tall and skinny—like a "bean pole," Aunt Betty says. I have bigger feet than anyone I know, and that includes my mom. To make things worse, my teeth stick out so much that I'm going to have to get braces on them next year.

When I said that, my mother stopped her work and turned around to look at me. "Rebecca," she asked, "how can you even think such a thing? You were the cutest baby I have ever seen in my whole life. Don't you remember all those darling pictures in your baby book?"

I remembered. I also remembered that many of them were pictures of me crying. That brings to my mind another possibility. Aunt Betty is always talking about what a fussy baby I was. She says that even when I was tiny, I would not eat my vegetables. As fast as my mom could spoon them into my mouth, I would spit them back out.

"I'll bet she didn't want me because I was such a bad baby," I said slowly, "always crying and making trouble for everyone."

Just then the timer on the stove started to buzz. The brownies were done. Mom took them out of the oven and cut them into neat little squares. She put the biggest and crunchiest one on a plate and brought it to me. Then she pulled up a chair and sat down beside me.

"Rebecca," Mom said, "your birth mother's decision to allow you to be adopted had nothing at all to do with what kind of a baby you were. That decision was made before you were born. She didn't have a chance to get to know you. In fact, it is very likely that she never even saw you. If she didn't know you, and probably didn't even see you, how could she possibly be disappointed with you for any reason at all? Anyway, Rebecca, you were a wonderful baby, wonderful in every way. And you have grown into a wonderful young lady. Your father and I are very proud of you, and we love you very much. We would not trade you for anyone else in the whole world!"

For a while I didn't say anything. I kept busy munching my hot brownie. Maybe my mother was right. If what she said was true, it really could not have been my fault that I was given up. What a relief that was!

After I finished the last crumbs of my brownie and my last swallow of milk, I said, "But, Mom, if the reason wasn't me, then what could it have been?"

"I know more about Mark's birth mother than I know about yours," Mom said. "Mark was older when we got him. His caseworker told us a lot about him. His birth mother tried to keep him, but she was too young to be a good mother. She was only fifteen years old, you see, and she was still in high school. She just could not earn enough money to support herself and a tiny baby, too. So she decided it would be better for everyone if she allowed him to be adopted into a family that could raise him properly. It is very possible, Rebecca, that your birth mother was in the same situation."

"Well, I wish I knew!" I said.

"So do I," Mom said. "I am sorry now that I didn't get more information from your caseworker when I had the chance.

211

It is just that you were so little that I never stopped to think that the time would come when you would want to know things like this.

"But even though we don't know your birth mother's actual reason for giving you up, we can be certain of one thing. She must have agreed with Dad and me that it is important for you to grow up in a family with two parents who really love you and can give you a good home. Whatever her reason may have been, she surely knew that she was unable to give you the kind of a home that she knew you needed. That is why she arranged for you to be adopted by a family who could. It was important to her to know that you would be happy and well cared for."

"Do you think it was hard for her to give me up?" I asked.

"I am sure of it," Mom said. "It was probably the hardest thing she ever had to do in her whole life. It must have been a very, very sad time for her. But do you know what? God used her terribly sad situation to answer your father's and my greatest prayer. He brought you into our family."

I guess my birth mother did the best thing she could do for me. I am really glad that she didn't decide to keep me when she knew that she could not take good care of me. And I surely am glad that God had a home for me to go to—a home where I am greatly wanted and loved, a home where I really belong.

Sometimes it is fun to imagine what I will be like when I am grown up. If I close my eyes I can almost see it. I will meet a really nice man, who I can love forever. And he will love me, too, of course. He will be a Christian so that we can pray together and ask God to guide our lives, just like my mom and dad. We will get married and have children, or maybe we will adopt them. I am not sure about that.

But there is one thing I *am* sure about. I am sure that I will never, ever get myself into a sad situation as my birth mother did. I never want to have to make the decision to give up my baby.

4. Am I Really So Special?

From the time I can first remember, people have been telling me how special I am. They still tell me that. I think they probably say the same thing to all adopted kids.

Some people say that our whole family is special and that is why God put us together in a special way. That probably sounds good to them, but I am not so sure I like it. I don't think I want to be that special. You know what it sounds like to me? It sounds like they are saying I am different from other kids, and I don't want to be different.

Lots of people say that adopted kids are "chosen" kids. Since the word "chosen" means "picked out," I always thought that was exactly what had happened—that my mom and dad had actually picked me out. I imagined that they went downtown to a big building with lots of rooms filled with baby cribs. In each crib was a tiny, newborn baby. There were babies of all kinds there—baby boys and baby girls, black babies and white babies, Indian babies and oriental babies, little ones and big ones, noisy ones and quiet ones. People could walk through all the different rooms and search through the babies until they found one that they wanted to adopt.

I imagined that my parents searched and searched, but they just couldn't find a baby that was exactly right for them. Then, tucked into a little crib over in a corner, they saw me. I was just what they wanted! So they checked me out and took me home with them.

Now doesn't that sound to you like the way a child would be chosen? Well, it isn't. But I didn't find that out until a couple of years ago. The truth is that my parents did not really choose *me* at all. Oh, they did choose to adopt a baby, all right, but not *me*. I just happened to be the one they got.

To tell the truth, it was sort of a relief to find out that I was not chosen the way I had always imagined. Being a chosen child isn't easy, you know. I always felt that I had to be exactly what my mom and dad wanted me to be. What I wanted didn't matter at all.

Even worse, I was always afraid of what might happen to me. I admit that there are many times when I disappoint my parents. I am not even close to being a perfect kid. What if my parents decided that they were sorry that they had chosen me? They just might make up their minds to take me back and choose someone else—someone they liked better.

There is another thing, too. Although I have always loved the stories about those special Bible people that my grandmother told me about—you know, Samuel and Joseph and Moses and Esther—they worried me, too. Those people were special, and they were chosen just as I was supposed to be. The problem is, every one of them did wonderful things with their lives. But what about me? I don't think that I will ever be important as they were. I hope people don't expect me to be. If they do, I'm afraid that they are going to be awfully disappointed.

For a long time I have worried and wondered about this. Finally I decided to do what I should have done in the first place: talk it over with my mom and dad.

"People are always saying that I'm special," I said, "but I'm not sure I really understand what they mean. Do you think I am special?"

"Of course we do, Rebecca," said Dad. "You are very special. You are special to our family, and you are special to God. But there is something that you must understand. Every child in the whole entire world is special, too. There may be people who are not loved by a single person on earth, but even they are special to God. That is why God sent His Son, Jesus, to earth, so that everyone would have a chance to become one of God's children. And for everyone who loves God and becomes His child through Jesus, God has a special place in His plan."

That is just what I needed to hear. Although I don't want

to be any more special than other kids, I surely don't want to be any less special, either.

"But what about being 'chosen'?" I asked. "I know that you and Mom didn't really choose me, but people still call me a 'chosen child.'"

"And they are right," Dad said. "It is true that Mom and I were unable to choose a specific child to adopt. We could not do that, but God could. So we depended on Him to do the choosing for us. And we are so glad and thankful that you are the one He chose."

"Do you mean that God chose me the same way He chose Moses and Esther and Samuel and Joseph?" I asked doubtfully.

"He sure did," Dad said. "Exactly the same way. God chose you to love Him and to do the job He has for you to do. Of course that doesn't mean that He will give you the same kind of a job that He gave them. God doesn't give history-changing jobs like theirs to very many people, you know. He may have chosen you to be a teacher or a lawyer or a missionary, or maybe He chose you to be a veterinarian or a secretary. Maybe He wants you to be a homemaker like your mom. You see, Rebecca, the particular job that God gives you to do isn't what is really important. The important thing is whether or not you are ready and willing to do whatever it is that God wants you to do."

I like the way my dad explains things. Maybe being "special" and "chosen" are not so bad after all. In fact, I have noticed a funny thing. Lots of times I hear kids say that they wish they were adopted too! They say that then they would know for sure that their parents really wanted them. Maybe instead of only telling us adopted kids how special we are, people should be saying it to all kids. Maybe then everyone could feel special and chosen.

I am a chosen child. God chose me, and He made me a part of just the right family. I am also a very special person—special to my family and special to God. This is just the way I like it!

5. *Where Do I Go From Here?*

"If I were adopted, I'd want to find the people I was born to," Linda told me one day.

"Why?" I asked.

"So that I could see who they are and what they look like," she said.

I didn't say anything.

"Why don't you try to find your birth mother?" Linda asked. "That would be so exciting!"

I couldn't think of anything else to say, so I said, "If I ever did find her, I wouldn't know what to say."

In some ways I think Linda is right. Finding my birth mother does sound pretty exciting. Linda is not the only one who has suggested it to me, either. Some of my other friends have said the same thing. Even my Aunt Betty talked to me about it once.

When I asked my brother if he ever wanted to search for his birth parents, he said, "No way! Mom and Dad are the only parents I care about. I am happy with things just the way the way they are. Why would I want to cause any problems?"

I should have known Mark would say that. He is never curious about anything.

"Even if I did know my birth parents, it wouldn't change the way I feel about Mom and Dad," I explained to him. "They would still be my real parents, and they will always be the ones I love. Nothing will ever change that."

"But how would they know that?" Mark asked. "I mean, if you are really happy with them, why would you want to find some other parents?"

That is a good question, and I really don't know the answer to it. I guess it's just that I am curious. It seems as if I am always wondering things—such as, does my birth mother look like me, skinny with sticking-out teeth, or is she beautiful? Was she awful in math when she was a kid? Does she play the piano or the flute as I do? I suppose questions like these don't seem very important to other people, but they are things that I just can't help wondering.

But there is another thing. If I ever did find out who my birth mother is and where she lives, I don't have the slightest idea what I would do about it. I mean, it would be pretty awful just to walk up and knock on her door. She probably would not even let me in. Why should she? After all, I am a complete stranger to her.

Of course, I would not actually have to go and see her. I could just write her a letter and tell her that I am happy with my family and that I am glad that she didn't keep me if she couldn't give me a good home. But then, what good would that do me? None of my questions would be answered. I would end up just as curious as ever.

"Would your mom and dad be mad if you wanted to find your first mother?" Linda asked me.

I said I didn't know. I had never asked them.

"Well, why don't you ask them?" Linda said.

And I said, "I just might do that."

But the truth is, I was afraid to ask them. What if they thought I didn't love them any more? Or what if they felt that I didn't think they were good enough parents to me? I for sure did not want to hurt their feelings. I would not do that for anything in the world. So instead of coming right out and saying anything to my mom and dad, I just hinted around.

One time I said, "I saw a lady at the store today who sort of looked like me. I wonder if she could be related to me— maybe an aunt or something."

Another time I said to my mom, "It isn't fair for you to make me eat broccoli. It's not my fault that I hate it. My taste buds probably take after my birth parents. If I ever meet them,

I am going to ask if they like broccoli, and I will bet they say no!"

I guess my mom got the idea, because she finally said, "Rebecca, I can understand your curiosity about your birth parents, about who they were and what they were like. If you have any questions you want to ask me about them, go ahead and ask. I don't mind at all. If I know the answers I will tell you. Unfortunately, though, I don't know very much. I wish I did, but I just don't."

"There are lots of times when I have questions, Mom," I said. "But I'm afraid that my questions will make you and Dad feel bad, and I don't want to do that."

"Your questions won't make us feel bad, Rebecca," Mom said. "You have a right to be curious. I certainly would be curious if I were you. I just wish that I had more information to give you."

I wish she did, too. I would really like to know what those other people were like.

When I was little I had some very strange ideas. I was sure that my birth parents were something really special—rich or famous or very important. I even thought that I might be a long lost princess or the child of some rich movie stars. I thought that I never was really given up in the first place, but that I had been kidnapped when I was a baby and given to the adoption agency. Now that I am older I know how silly that was. I suppose that if I ever do meet those people I will be disappointed at how ordinary they are.

I have seen television programs about people who actually did find their birth parents. In those shows the people always end up living happily-ever-after. But of course, those stories are just make-believe and that is the way most make-believe stories end. In real life, though, I don't think it would work out like that very often.

Mark read a story in the newspaper about a girl in college who spent years searching for her birth mother. Finally she found her. The girl was really excited, and she made a lot of plans for all the happy times she and her birth mother would have together. But things didn't work out at all the way she had planned. The woman was married by this time, you see, and she had three little children. When the girl called her on the phone, the woman got really angry, because she didn't want her husband and children to find out about that other daughter. She said that if the girl came around, it would ruin her whole life and that it was cruel and unfair for the girl ever to have searched her out in the first place. The woman told the girl never to call her again and never, ever to try to see her.

In the end the girl was very sad and very hurt. She said she wished that she had never started that search in the first place. Mark says it served her right for not being satisfied with things the way they were. I feel sorry for her anyway. I know how curious kids can get.

Probably my birth mother has a happy new life by now, too. She probably has a husband and children who she can love and who will love her back. I hope so. If that is true, she certainly would not want me coming back and messing things up for her. It would not be fair for me to do that. When she gave me up, she gave me up for good.

Since God knows everything way before it happens, how could He possibly make mistakes? He couldn't! And since He doesn't make mistakes, then He must have put me where I belong, and that's right here with my mom and my dad and my brother. If I am already where I belong, then why would I need to know those other people from way back in my beginning?

There are still things that I wonder about, but it is only because I am curious. I don't want to find a new mother. I like my old one just fine. And I don't ever want to take the chance of making her think that she has not been a good enough mother to me, because she has.

I guess what I am saying is that I have got the very best parents right now. Why would I want to find any others?

6. *What Do Other Kids Say?*

Last summer the Johnson family moved into our neighborhood. Pretty soon they started coming to our church. They have two kids—Michelle, who is one year older than I, and Jeff, who is one year younger than I. I did not know them very well, but I knew that they were adopted. They talked about it all the time.

One morning at breakfast Mom told Mark and me that Mrs. Johnson was worried about Michelle and Jeff. Mom said Mrs. Johnson told her that they were having some kind of problems. Mrs. Johnson said it was probably because her kids were adopted.

"So what if they are adopted?" I asked. "What does that have to do with anything?"

"Mrs. Johnson seems to think that adopted children have a lot more problems than other children do," Mom explained. "She is hoping that you two can help Michelle and Jeff."

"Us?" said Mark. "What can we do?" He was talking with his mouth full again, but Mom didn't scold him.

"Once a week Michelle and Jeff have been meeting with Dr. Reed, the counselor at church," Mom said. "He has been trying to help them to understand and work out their problems. Dr. Reed thinks that if they had a chance to share their concerns with other adopted children, it might help them. At his suggestion Mrs. Johnson has invited you two—and also Steven Taylor—to meet with her children in Dr. Reed's office."

Mark didn't want to go until Mom told him that if he went, he wouldn't have to do any of his Saturday jobs. Then he suddenly decided that it wasn't such a bad idea after all.

The very next week we all got together. Dr. Reed was there, but he didn't talk much. Mark was the oldest one of the kids, and Michelle was next oldest. Steven is the same age as me, so

Jeff was the youngest. Dr. Reed had the room set up with chairs for all of us, and Mrs. Johnson brought a bunch of popcorn and soda pop for everyone.

Dr. Reed started us off by asking if we thought adopted kids had more problems than other kids. Mark said no. Michelle and Jeff said yes. Steven said, "Everyone has problems. The thing is, adopted kids just have one more thing to think about." I agreed with Steven.

"It's more than that!" Michelle said in an angry voice. "Sometimes I feel like I am not even wanted at home. I don't really belong. Sometimes I feel like I am living with a houseful of strangers!"

I couldn't understand that at all. My family never seems like strangers to me.

"How can you feel that you are not wanted?" Mark asked her. "Your parents didn't *have* to adopt you, you know."

"But that doesn't mean they love me as much as they would if I had been born to them," Michelle said.

"I think I know what you mean," said Steven. "My little sister was born to my parents, and sometimes I can't help wondering if they love her more than they love me."

"I just wish I could know for positive sure that my parents do love me and accept me just as much as they would if I had been born their child," Michelle said.

I asked Michelle why she didn't just ask them.

She said, "Oh, I couldn't do that!"

I asked her why not. "That's what I would do. My mom says it's O.K. to wonder about things. She says she would wonder, too, if she were me."

"I always wonder things," said Jeff. "The thing I wonder about the most is my birth parents. Sometimes I wonder if they ever think about me and wonder how I am."

"Well," I said, "even if you do ask your parents, you probably won't get all the answers you want, because they won't know all the answers."

Then Michelle said, "One of the things I wonder about is

why I was given up in the first place. I think it was probably because I'm ugly."

I couldn't believe Michelle was saying that. She's really a pretty girl. If only I looked like her! So I asked, "Why do you think you're ugly, Michelle?"

She said, "Because a girl at school told me so. She said, 'No wonder your birth mother gave you up. You were too ugly to keep!' "

"What do you care what she says?" Mark asked. "What does she know about it? I'll bet she was just teasing you."

"Probably so," Michelle said. "Kids are always teasing me about being adopted. One time a boy in my class said, 'I'll bet you had to be adopted because when you were born you were so ugly that your mother died of fright as soon as she saw you.' Lots of other kids have said that it is obvious that I wasn't good enough for my birth mother or she would have kept me."

"The same thing happens to me sometimes," said Jeff. "One time one of my friends got really mad at me, and he said that I was ugly and stupid and no wonder I was adopted."

"How come everyone knows that you are adopted?" Mark asked Michelle and Jeff. "You must talk about it all the time."

"So what if we talk about it?" said Jeff.

"So you are just giving the other kids something else to tease you about," Mark said.

"Everyone gets teased about something," Steven said. "If it's not about being adopted, then it's about having freckles or being dumb in math or being fat."

"Or about sticking-out teeth," I said. "The boys in my class call me 'beaver mouth.' I hate it!"

"Well, I would rather be teased about that kind of stuff than about being adopted," Michelle said.

"Then don't talk so much about being adopted. Then they *will* tease you about other stuff," said Mark. He was starting to sound sort of disgusted, the way he sometimes does with me.

"Adopted kids have lots of other problems, too," Michelle said, "like not feeling loved as much as kids who are born to their parents. Or feeling as if you are not as good as other kids. Or not getting along with your parents all that well."

"What is so special about those problems?" Mark asked. "Lots of my friends who are not even adopted say those very same things. You probably just think that they are special problems for adopted kids because you are adopted and those are the problems you are having."

"When things bother me, I talk them over with my mom and dad," I said. "Sometimes they can't help me, but most of the time they can."

"Not me!" Michelle said. "My parents are the ones who *cause* a lot of *my* problems. It seems as if they want to control my whole life. What I can't understand is, why do they have to worry all the time? What is wrong with me that they can't just leave me alone?"

"If you think Michelle talks a lot about being adopted, you should hear our mom," said Jeff. "She talks about it *all* the time, to *everyone*. I just wish she didn't have to always make such a big deal out of it."

"Maybe she doesn't know it bothers you," I said. "You should tell her."

"But that might hurt her feelings," Jeff said. "I don't want to hurt her feelings."

"You could say it in a nice way," I suggested. "Not when you are angry or upset, just sometime when you are sitting around together. It really isn't fair to be angry with her about something that you have not told her bothers you."

"At least your mother is not afraid to talk about your being adopted," Steven said. "I know a boy whose parents never even told him. They just pretended he had been born to them. Then one day his cousin told him the truth. He was so surprised that he didn't believe it at first. Then he was really, really angry."

"I'd be angry, too!" Jeff said. "That's just like lying. Kids don't like parents who lie to them."

"If parents would lie about something as important as that,

how could their kids believe anything they say?" Steven questioned.

"I guess since I am adopted I am glad that I know the truth," Michelle said. "But what I really wish is that I wasn't an adopted kid in the first place."

"Maybe that is why you are sometimes so mean to Mom and Dad," Jeff said to Michelle.

"Well, being adopted really upsets me!" said Michelle.

I believe her. She surely did sound upset to me.

"If you were not adopted, where would you be now?" Mark asked Michelle.

That seemed like a pretty good question. I was wondering the same thing.

"You might not have a family at all," Mark told her. "Or at least you might not have one that loves you and can give you all the things you need."

"I think adopted kids should be glad they are adopted," Steven said. "Being adopted proves that your parents really wanted you. You didn't just happen to fall into your family, you know. They had to work hard to get you."

"I think that the most important thing is to be able to talk your problems over with your parents," Mark said. "Even if they can't give you answers, they can at least listen to you and find out what is bothering you. It will make them feel good to know that you want their opinion. Maybe if you talked to your mom more, she would not worry so much about you. That would solve one of your problems right there."

Then Mark said, "That's what families are for, you know: to listen to and to help each other whenever they can."

Sometimes Mark surely is smart. You know what? I am really glad that he is my brother. And I am really glad that I am a part of my family. In fact, I am glad I am part of both of my families—my mom and dad's family, and God's family. What more could I ask?